Managing Stress In The Modern World:

Practical Techniques for a Balanced Life

Dr Robert E. Wright

Table of Contents

Introduction: Understanding Stress In The Modern World

In today's fast-paced and interconnected world, the experience of stress has become an all too familiar companion in our lives. The demands of modern living, ranging from professional responsibilities to personal obligations, can often leave us feeling overwhelmed, exhausted, and mentally stretched. This introduction serves as a foundational exploration into the intricate nature of stress and its profound impact on our physical, mental, and emotional well-being.

The Impact of Stress on Health and Well-being

Stress can have a significant impact on both our physical health and general well-being. When the body experiences stress, it triggers a complex physiological response known as the "fight or flight" response, which is a natural survival mechanism. While this response is essential in emergency situations, prolonged or chronic stress can lead to various negative effects on health and well-being.

1. Physical Health Impact:

- **Cardiovascular System**: Chronic stress can contribute to high blood pressure, an increased heart rate, and a higher risk of heart disease.

- **Immune System**: Stress weakens the immune system, making the body more susceptible to infections and illnesses.

- **Digestive System**: Stress can lead to digestive problems such as irritable bowel syndrome (IBS), indigestion, and appetite changes.

- **Weight Management**: Stress may influence weight gain or loss due to changes in appetite, overeating, or undereating.

- **Sleep Disruption**: Stress can cause sleep disturbances, leading to insomnia or poor sleep quality.

- **Musculoskeletal Issues**: Tense muscles and prolonged stress can contribute to muscle pain, tension headaches, and body aches.

2. Mental and Emotional Impact:

- **Anxiety and Depression**: Chronic stress is linked to an increased risk of anxiety disorders and depression.

- **Cognitive Function**: High stress levels can impair concentration, memory, decision-making, and overall cognitive function.
- **Emotional Well-Being**: Stress can lead to mood swings, irritability, and a reduced ability to manage emotions effectively.

- **Burnout**: Prolonged stress can lead to burnout, which is characterized by emotional exhaustion and a decreased sense of accomplishment.

3. Behavior and Lifestyle Impact:

- **Unhealthy Coping Mechanisms**: People under stress may resort to unhealthy coping mechanisms such as smoking, excessive alcohol consumption, or overeating.

- **Physical Inactivity**: Stress can lead to reduced motivation for physical activity, impacting overall fitness and well-being.

- **Impaired Relationships**: High stress levels can strain relationships due to irritability, decreased communication, and emotional distancing.

- **Work Performance**: Chronic stress may affect job performance, productivity, and job satisfaction.

4. General Well-Being:

- **Quality of Life**: Prolonged stress can negatively impact the overall quality of life, affecting happiness, contentment, and life satisfaction.

- **Social Engagement**: High stress levels can lead to social isolation and reduced participation in social and recreational activities.

- **Sense of Purpose**: Chronic stress can challenge one's sense of purpose and hinder personal growth and development.

Recognizing the impact of stress on both physical health and general well-being underscores the importance of effective stress management techniques. By adopting strategies to reduce and manage stress, individuals can enhance their overall quality of life, improve health outcomes, and cultivate a sense of balance and resilience in the face of life's challenges.

Recognizing The Sources of Modern Stressors

- **Identifying Key Triggers:**

Here's an overview of some of the key triggers of stress that many individuals experience:

- **Workplace Demands and Pressure**: Job-related stress is a common trigger. High workloads, tight deadlines, demanding bosses, and the pressure to perform can contribute to significant stress levels.

- **Financial Concerns**: Worries about money, debt, bills, and financial stability can lead to persistent stress and anxiety.

- **Relationship Struggles**: Difficulties in personal relationships, whether with a partner, family members, or friends, can create emotional strain and stress.

- **Health Issues**: Dealing with chronic illnesses, medical diagnoses, or the health concerns of loved ones can be emotionally taxing and contribute to stress.

- **Life Transitions**: Major life changes such as moving, changing jobs, getting married, or having a baby can disrupt routines and cause stress.

- **Academic Pressure**: Students often face stress from academic performance, exams, assignments, and the expectations of teachers or parents.

- **Time Management**: Feeling overwhelmed by a lack of time to accomplish tasks and meet commitments can lead to stress.

- **Technology and Information Overload**: Constant connectivity, social media pressures, and information overload can contribute to a feeling of overwhelm and stress.

- **Environmental Factors**: Noise, pollution, and other environmental stressors can impact well-being.

- **Social Comparison and Peer Pressure**: Comparing oneself to others and feeling pressure to meet social norms or expectations can be stressful.

- **Personal Expectations**: Setting overly high standards for oneself, perfectionism, and fear of failure can lead to chronic stress.

- **Loss and Grief**: Dealing with the loss of a loved one or experiencing grief can cause profound stress and emotional turmoil.

- **Uncertainty and Change**: Dealing with the unknown, unexpected changes, and ambiguous situations can trigger stress.

- **Trauma and Past Experiences**: Previous traumatic events or experiences can have a lasting impact on mental and emotional well-being, leading to ongoing stress.

It's important to note that individuals may experience stress differently based on their unique circumstances and coping mechanisms. Additionally, some level of stress is a natural response to challenges and changes in life. The goal is not to eliminate stress entirely but to develop effective strategies for managing and mitigating its impact on overall well-being. The techniques and insights presented in your book can provide valuable tools for addressing these key triggers of stress and promoting a more balanced and resilient life.

- **External vs. Internal Stressors: Unraveling the Web**

Understanding the distinction between external and internal stressors is crucial for identifying and managing sources of stress. Here's an explanation of both types:

External Stressors:

External stressors are factors that originate from the outside environment and contribute to feelings of stress. These stressors are often tangible and observable, making them easier to identify. External stressors can include:

- **Workplace Demands**: High workloads, tight deadlines, excessive responsibilities, and challenging work environments can all lead to stress.

- **Financial Pressures**: Money-related worries such as debt, bills, job insecurity, and financial instability can significantly contribute to stress.

- **Relationship Issues**: Difficulties with family members, friends, colleagues, or romantic partners can create emotional stress.

- **Life Changes**: Major life transitions, such as moving to a new location, changing jobs, or experiencing significant personal changes, can be stressful.

- **Environmental Factors**: Noise, pollution, overcrowding, and other environmental conditions can impact stress levels.

- **Technology Overload**: The constant connectivity of modern technology, along with the pressure to be online and responsive, can be a significant external stressor.

Internal Stressors:

Internal stressors are factors that originate from within an individual's thoughts, beliefs, and emotions. They are more subjective and may not always be as obvious as external stressors. Internal stressors can include:

- **Negative Self-Talk**: Critical self-judgment, self-doubt, and a negative internal dialogue can lead to significant internal stress.

- **Perfectionism**: Setting unrealistically high standards for oneself and feeling intense pressure to meet them can be a major internal stressor.

- **Worry and Anxiety**: Constant worrying, excessive rumination, and chronic anxiety contribute to internal stress.

- **Self-Imposed Expectations**: Placing undue pressure on oneself to excel, perform, or meet certain standards can lead to internal stress.

- **Fear of Failure**: An intense fear of making mistakes or failing can cause significant internal stress.

- **Cognitive Distortions**: Distorted thinking patterns, such as catastrophizing or black-and-white thinking, can contribute to internal stress.

- **Negative Emotions**: Unresolved anger, resentment, guilt, and other negative emotions can create internal stress.

Understanding the interplay between external and internal stressors is essential for effective stress management. While external stressors may be beyond an individual's control, developing strategies to manage internal stressors can lead to improved well-being. Techniques such as Mindfulness, cognitive restructuring, self-compassion, and stress reduction practices can help individuals address both types of stressors and achieve a more balanced and resilient life.

- ## Cultural and Societal Factors Contributing to Contemporary Stress

Cultural and societal factors play a significant role in shaping contemporary stress levels by influencing perceptions, expectations, and behaviors. Here are some key cultural and societal factors that contribute to stress in the modern world:

1. Social Comparison and Self-Image:

- **Social Media Influence**: Constant exposure to curated images and posts on social media platforms can lead to feelings of inadequacy and the pressure to conform to unrealistic standards.

- **Comparison Culture**: A culture of comparison, where individuals gauge their success and worth based on others' achievements, can lead to chronic stress and anxiety.

2. High Achievement Expectations:

- **Cultural Values**: Societies that emphasize high achievement, success, and competition can foster a constant drive to excel, potentially leading to stress and burnout.

- **Academic and Career Pressure**: Expectations to excel academically or professionally can create intense stress, especially in cultures where prestige and status are highly valued.

3. Work-Life Imbalance:

- **Career-Centric Societies**: Societies that prioritize work and career success may contribute to a lack of balance between work and personal life, leading to increased stress and decreased well-being.

- **Limited Work Benefits**: Inadequate access to paid leave, flexible work arrangements, and support systems can contribute to work-related stress.

4. Cultural Norms and Gender Roles:

- **Gender Expectations**: Societal expectations related to gender roles and responsibilities can lead to stress when individuals feel pressure to fulfill traditional roles that may not align with their personal aspirations.

- **Family and Caregiving Pressures**: Balancing work, family, and caregiving responsibilities can create significant stress, particularly when societal norms dictate certain roles.

5. Financial and Economic Pressures:

- **Consumer Culture**: Societies that prioritize materialism and conspicuous consumption can lead to financial strain as individuals strive to meet societal expectations.

- **Income Inequality**: Economic disparities and financial instability can contribute to stress among those facing financial hardships.

6. Urbanization and Overstimulation:

- **Fast-Paced Lifestyle**: Urban environments characterized by noise, congestion, and constant activity can contribute to sensory overload and stress.

- **Information Overload**: The rapid flow of information in urbanized societies can lead to cognitive overload and heightened stress levels.

7. Cultural Stigma and Mental Health:

- **Stigmatization**: Societal stigma surrounding mental health issues can discourage individuals from seeking help, leading to increased stress and the potential exacerbation of mental health conditions.

8. Changing Family Dynamics:

- **Nuclear Families**: Shifts from extended family structures to nuclear families can create unique stressors, such as limited support systems and increased caregiving responsibilities.

Recognizing these cultural and societal factors is essential for understanding the broader context in which stressors emerge. By acknowledging and addressing these influences, individuals can develop more effective strategies for managing stress and fostering well-being in the modern world.

Why Managing Stress is Essential for a Balanced Life

Managing stress is essential for achieving and maintaining a balanced life for several important reasons:

1. Physical Health: Chronic stress can take a toll on your physical well-being. It has been linked to a range of health issues, including heart disease, high blood pressure, immune system suppression, digestive problems, and even an increased risk of certain chronic illnesses. By managing stress, you can significantly reduce the risk of these health problems and promote overall physical well-being.

2. Mental and Emotional Well-being: Unmanaged stress can contribute to the development of mental health conditions such as anxiety and depression. It can also exacerbate existing conditions. Effective stress management techniques can improve emotional resilience, boost mood, and enhance overall mental well-being.

3. Cognitive Function: High stress levels can impair cognitive function, leading to difficulties with concentration, memory, decision-making, and problem-solving. Managing stress helps maintain optimal cognitive abilities, allowing you to perform better in various aspects of life.

4. Relationships: Stress can strain relationships with family, friends, and colleagues. It may lead to irritability, conflict, and reduced communication. By managing stress, you can improve your interpersonal interactions, fostering healthier and more positive relationships.

5. Productivity and Performance: Excessive stress can hinder productivity and performance in various areas of life, including work and personal projects. Managing stress improves focus, creativity, and efficiency, leading to better outcomes and accomplishments.

6. Quality of Life: Chronic stress can diminish your overall quality of life by limiting your ability to engage in enjoyable activities and pursue personal interests. Effective stress management allows you to make the most of life's experiences, increasing your sense of fulfillment and happiness.

7. Longevity: Stress management is associated with increased longevity. By reducing stress-related health risks, you're more likely to live a longer, healthier life.
8. Resilience and Adaptability: Learning to manage stress enhances your ability to cope with challenges, setbacks, and unexpected changes. This resilience is invaluable in navigating life's uncertainties and maintaining a sense of equilibrium.

9. Self-Care and Well-Being: Prioritizing stress management is an act of self-care. It demonstrates a commitment to your own health and well-being, allowing you to lead a more fulfilling and balanced life.

10. Personal Growth: Managing stress fosters personal growth by encouraging self-awareness, emotional intelligence, and effective coping strategies. It provides opportunities for learning and self-improvement.

In essence, managing stress is a fundamental aspect of achieving and maintaining balance in all areas of your life. It empowers you to lead a healthier, happier, and more fulfilling existence, enabling you to navigate challenges with resilience and embrace life's opportunities with greater enthusiasm.

Chapter 1: Mind-Body Connection: Nurturing Your Well-being

This chapter explores the profound link between your mental state and your physical health. By nurturing this connection, you can enhance your overall well-being. Techniques like mindfulness and meditation help you stay present, while stress-reducing foods and exercise positively impact your mood. Prioritizing restorative sleep and holistic practices further strengthens your mind-body synergy, enabling you to manage stress, boost resilience, and create a balanced and fulfilling life.

Mindfulness and meditation are powerful practices that can profoundly impact your mental, emotional, and physical well-being. Let's delve a little deeper into the significance of mindfulness and meditation:

1.1 The Power of Mindfulness and Meditation

- **Mindfulness:**

Mindfulness is the practice of being fully present in the moment, observing your thoughts, feelings, and sensations without judgment. It involves cultivating awareness and acceptance of your experiences as they arise. This practice has gained widespread recognition for its ability to reduce stress, enhance self-awareness, and promote emotional regulation.

Benefits of Mindfulness:

- **Stress Reduction**: Mindfulness helps you detach from stressors and become an impartial observer of your thoughts. This can lead to reduced reactivity to stress and a calmer overall demeanor.

- **Emotional Regulation**: By acknowledging and accepting your emotions without judgment, mindfulness enables you to respond to challenging situations more skillfully and with greater emotional balance.

- **Improved Focus and Concentration**: Regular mindfulness practice enhances your ability to stay present and concentrate, leading to increased productivity and a clearer mind.

- **Enhanced Self-Awareness**: Mindfulness fosters a deeper understanding of your thoughts, habits, and reactions, allowing you to make conscious choices and cultivate personal growth.

- **Relationship Improvement**: Mindful presence in interactions promotes active listening, empathy, and effective communication, leading to more meaningful and harmonious relationships.

- **Meditation:**

Meditation involves intentionally focusing your mind to achieve a heightened state of awareness, relaxation, and clarity. There are various forms of meditation, each with unique benefits, but they generally share the goal of calming the mind and promoting inner peace.

- **Stress Reduction**: Meditation encourages a state of relaxation and activates the body's relaxation response, counteracting the effects of stress hormones.

- **Anxiety and Depression Management**: Regular meditation has been shown to reduce symptoms of anxiety and depression by fostering a sense of calm and promoting positive emotional states.

- **Mind-Body Connection**: Meditation strengthens the mind-body connection, allowing you to better understand and influence the body's reactions to stress and other stimuli.

- **Increased Resilience**: Meditation cultivates mental resilience, enabling you to cope with life's challenges and setbacks with greater equanimity.

- **Mindful Eating and Habits**: Mindful eating, a form of meditation, encourages conscious awareness of your relationship with food and can lead to healthier eating habits.

3. Incorporating Mindfulness and Meditation:

Regular practice is key to reaping the benefits of mindfulness and meditation. These practices can be integrated into daily life through formal sessions and informal moments of mindfulness. Whether through guided meditations, focused breathing exercises, or mindful activities like walking, eating, or even washing dishes, the consistent cultivation of mindfulness and meditation can lead to a more balanced, resilient, and fulfilling life.

1.2 Cultivating Self-Compassion and Self-Care

Practicing self-compassion and self-care is essential for nurturing your emotional well-being and building resilience. Here's how you can cultivate these qualities:

1. Self-Compassion:

Self-compassion involves treating yourself with the same kindness and understanding that you would offer a close friend. It means being gentle with yourself during difficult times and recognizing that imperfections are a natural part of being human.

- **Mindful Self-Awareness**: Notice when you're being self-critical or judgmental. Pause and acknowledge these thoughts without self-condemnation. Remember that everyone experiences challenges and mistakes.

- **Kind Self-Talk**: Replace harsh self-talk with kind and supportive words. Treat yourself with the same warmth and understanding that you would extend to a loved one.

- **Common Humanity**: Recognize that you're not alone in your struggles. Others also face difficulties and make mistakes. This shared humanity helps create a sense of connection and understanding.

- **Self-Compassion Breaks**: During moments of stress or self-criticism, take a self-compassion break. Acknowledge your feelings, remind yourself that suffering is a part of life, and offer yourself words of kindness.

2. Self-Care:

Self-care involves intentionally prioritizing activities and practices that promote your physical, mental, and emotional well-being. It's a way of refueling and recharging to better cope with life's demands.

- **Identify Your Needs**: Reflect on what activities, hobbies, and practices bring you joy and relaxation. Consider your physical, emotional, and social needs.

- **Create a Routine**: Develop a consistent self-care routine that includes activities you enjoy, such as reading, spending time outdoors, practicing hobbies, or engaging in creative expression.

- **Set Boundaries**: Establish healthy boundaries to protect your time and energy. Learn to say no when necessary to prevent overcommitting and burnout.

- **Prioritize Rest**: Ensure you get enough sleep and practice good sleep hygiene. Quality rest is crucial for overall well-being.

- **Mindful Moments**: Incorporate moments of mindfulness throughout your day. Take short breaks to focus on your breath, ground yourself in the present, and alleviate stress.

- **Physical Health**: Engage in regular physical activity, eat a balanced diet, and stay hydrated. Caring for your body positively impacts your mental and emotional state.

- **Seek Support**: Don't hesitate to reach out to friends, family, or professionals when you need emotional support. Seeking help is a sign of strength.

Cultivating self-compassion and practicing self-care require consistent effort and patience. These practices empower you to be kind to yourself, prioritize your well-being, and develop the resilience needed to navigate life's challenges with grace and strength.

1.3 Integrating Physical Activity For Stress Relief

Integrating physical activity into your routine for stress relief can be highly effective. Physical exercise has been shown to reduce stress hormones, improve mood, and promote overall well-being. Here's how you can do it:

1. Choose Activities You Enjoy: Opt for exercises that you find enjoyable. Whether it's walking, jogging, swimming, dancing, cycling, yoga, or playing a sport, engaging in activities you like increases the likelihood of sticking with them.

2. Make it a Regular Habit: Consistency is key. Aim for at least 30 minutes of moderate-intensity exercise most days of the week. Establish a schedule that works for you and gradually build up your routine.

3. Mindful Movement: Engage in mindful exercise by focusing on your movements and sensations. Pay attention to your breath, the rhythm of your steps, or the stretch in your muscles. This can enhance the stress-relieving benefits of physical activity.

4. Outdoor Activities: Spending time in nature can provide a soothing and calming environment. Consider outdoor activities like hiking, nature walks, or jogging in a park to combine physical exercise with stress-reducing nature exposure.

5. Cardiovascular Exercise: Activities that get your heart rate up, such as brisk walking, running, cycling, or swimming, trigger the release of endorphins, natural chemicals that boost your mood and reduce stress.

6. Mind-Body Practices: Yoga, tai chi, and qigong combine physical movement with mindfulness and breath awareness. These practices promote relaxation, flexibility, and stress reduction.

7. Social Engagement: Join a sports club, exercise class, or recreational group to combine physical activity with social interaction, which can further enhance your well-being.

8. Breaks During the Day: Incorporate short bursts of physical activity throughout your day. Take a walk during breaks, do stretching exercises, or practice deep breathing to alleviate stress.

9. Progressive Muscle Relaxation: Combine relaxation techniques with physical activity. For example, you can tense and then release your muscles while walking or doing gentle stretches.

10. Dancing: Dancing not only provides a cardiovascular workout but also offers a creative outlet and an opportunity to express yourself. Dancing to your favorite music can be a joyful and stress-relieving activity.

Remember, the goal is to find physical activities that suit your preferences, abilities, and schedule. Gradually integrate exercise into your routine and pay attention to how it positively impacts your stress levels and overall well-being.

Chapter 2: Nutrition For Resilience: Fueling Your Body and Mind

The foods you consume play a crucial role in supporting your body's ability to manage stress and build resilience. A balanced and nutrient-rich diet can positively impact your mood, energy levels, and overall well-being. Here's how you can use nutrition to enhance your resilience to stress:

1. Balanced Meals:
Aim for balanced meals that include a variety of nutrient-dense foods. Incorporate a mix of lean proteins, whole grains, healthy fats, and a colorful array of fruits and vegetables.

2. Stress-Reducing Nutrients:
Certain nutrients can help reduce stress and support your nervous system. Consider including foods rich in B vitamins (whole grains, lean meats, nuts, seeds), magnesium (leafy greens, nuts, legumes), and omega-3 fatty acids (fatty fish, flaxseeds, walnuts).

3. Complex Carbohydrates:
Opt for complex carbohydrates like whole grains (brown rice, quinoa, and whole wheat) that provide sustained

energy and help stabilize blood sugar levels, reducing
mood swings and stress.

4. Hydration:
Staying hydrated is essential for optimal bodily
functions, including stress management. Drink plenty of
water throughout the day to support your overall well-
being.

5. Antioxidant-Rich Foods:
Antioxidants help combat oxidative stress, which can
contribute to chronic diseases and impact your response
to stress. Incorporate colorful fruits and vegetables
(berries, spinach, and bell peppers) as well as nuts and
seeds into your diet.

6. Gut-Brain Connection:
A healthy gut contributes to better mental well-being.
Consume probiotic-rich foods (yogurt, kefir, and
sauerkraut) and fiber to support gut health and promote a
balanced mood.

7. Limit Stimulants:
Limit caffeine and sugary foods, as excessive
consumption can lead to energy crashes and increased
stress levels.

8. Mindful Eating:
Practice mindful eating by savoring your meals and
paying attention to flavors and textures. This can help
reduce emotional eating and promote a healthier
relationship with food.

9. Regular Meals:
Aim to eat regular meals and snacks throughout the day
to maintain steady blood sugar levels and prevent energy
dips.

10. Moderation and Variety:
Enjoy a wide range of foods in moderation. A diverse
diet ensures you receive a broad spectrum of nutrients
that contribute to overall resilience.

11. **Adequate Protein Intake**:
Including sources of lean protein (chicken, fish, beans,
and lentils) in your diet supports the production of
neurotransmitters that regulate mood and stress.

Remember that nutrition is just one piece of the puzzle.
Combining a well-balanced diet with other stress
management techniques, such as exercise, mindfulness,
and social support, will contribute to your overall
resilience and well-being.

2.1 Stress-Reducing Foods and Nutrients

Stress-reducing foods and nutrients can have a
significant impact on your ability to manage stress and
promote overall well-being. These foods contain
compounds that support your nervous system, regulate
mood, and mitigate the physiological effects of stress.

Here are some key stress-reducing foods and nutrients to consider:

1. B Vitamins:

B vitamins, particularly B6, B9 (folate), and B12, are essential for the production of neurotransmitters like serotonin and dopamine, which play a role in mood regulation.
Food sources: Whole grains (oats, brown rice), lean meats (chicken, turkey), fish, legumes, leafy greens, nuts, and seeds.

2. Magnesium:

Magnesium helps relax muscles and supports a calm nervous system response.
Food sources: Leafy greens (spinach, kale), nuts (almonds, cashews), seeds (pumpkin, sunflower), whole grains, legumes, and dark chocolate.

3. Omega-3 Fatty Acids:

Omega-3s have anti-inflammatory properties and can help reduce cortisol, a stress hormone.
Food sources: Fatty fish (salmon, mackerel, and sardines), flaxseeds, chia seeds, and walnuts.

4. Vitamin C:

Vitamin C is an antioxidant that helps combat oxidative stress caused by chronic stress.
Food sources: Citrus fruits (oranges, grapefruits), berries (strawberries, blueberries), bell peppers, broccoli.

5. Complex Carbohydrates:
Complex carbs promote steady blood sugar levels,
reducing mood swings and stress-related energy crashes.
Food sources: Whole grains (quinoa, brown rice, whole
wheat), legumes, and starchy vegetables (sweet potatoes,
squash).

6. Serotonin-Promoting Foods:
Foods that contain tryptophan, an amino acid precursor
to serotonin, can help regulate mood and reduce anxiety.
Food sources: Turkey, chicken, nuts, seeds, tofu, dairy
products, bananas.

7. Probiotics:
A healthy gut microbiome supports brain health and
mood regulation.
Food sources: Fermented foods (yogurt, kefir,
sauerkraut, kimchi), kombucha.

8. Adaptogens:
Adaptogenic herbs like ashwagandha, rhodiola, and holy
basil may help the body adapt to stress and promote a
sense of calm.
These are often available in supplement form or as
herbal teas.

9. Herbal Teas:
Certain herbal teas, such as chamomile, lavender, and
lemon balm, have calming properties that can help
reduce stress and promote relaxation.

10. Dark Chocolate:

Dark chocolate contains flavonoids that have antioxidant and mood-enhancing effects. Enjoy in moderation for a delightful stress-relieving treat.

Incorporating these stress-reducing foods into your diet can contribute to a more balanced and resilient response to stress. Remember that no single food is a magic solution, but adopting a well-rounded diet that includes these nutrients can complement other stress management practices and contribute to your overall well-being.

2.2 The Gut-Brain Connection and Emotional Health

The gut-brain connection refers to the bidirectional communication between the gut (digestive system) and the brain. This intricate relationship has profound implications for emotional health, stress response, and overall well-being. Here's how the gut-brain connection works and its impact on emotional health:

1. The Gut-Brain Axis:
The gut-brain axis involves a complex network of signals and interactions between the gut, the central nervous system (CNS), and the enteric nervous system (ENS), which is sometimes referred to as the "second brain." The ENS controls the gastrointestinal system and operates independently while also communicating with the CNS.

2. Neurotransmitters and Mood Regulation:
The gut produces a significant amount of neurotransmitters, including serotonin, dopamine, and gamma-aminobutyric acid (GABA). These neurotransmitters play a crucial role in regulating mood, emotions, and stress responses. For example, about 90% of serotonin, often called the "feel-good" neurotransmitter, is produced in the gut.

3. Gut Microbiota:
The gut is home to trillions of microorganisms, collectively known as the gut microbiota. These microbes play a vital role in various physiological functions, including digestion, metabolism, and the immune response. Emerging research suggests that the gut microbiota can influence brain function and emotional health.

4. Inflammation and Immune Response:
A disrupted gut microbiota balance can lead to increased inflammation in the body. Chronic inflammation has been linked to mood disorders such as depression and anxiety. The immune response in the gut can also affect the central nervous system and impact emotional well-being.

5. Stress Response:
The gut-brain connection is closely intertwined with the body's stress response. Stress can affect gut function, leading to gastrointestinal symptoms, while gut health influences the body's ability to manage stress. The two-

way communication between the gut and the brain plays a role in regulating the stress response.

6. Emotions and Digestion:

Emotions can influence gut function and digestion. Stress and negative emotions can lead to symptoms like stomachaches, indigestion, and irritable bowel syndrome (IBS). Conversely, gastrointestinal discomfort can also impact mood and emotional well-being.

7. Gut-Brain Disorders:

Imbalances in the gut-brain connection have been associated with certain psychiatric and neurological conditions, including depression, anxiety, autism spectrum disorder, and more. Researchers are exploring how addressing gut health could complement traditional treatments for these conditions.

8. Dietary Impact:

Diet plays a significant role in shaping the gut microbiota and influencing the gut-brain connection. Consuming a diet rich in fiber, prebiotics, and probiotics can support a healthy gut microbiota and potentially positively impact emotional health.

Understanding and nurturing the gut-brain connection through a healthy diet, stress management, regular physical activity, and practices like mindfulness can contribute to improved emotional well-being. This connection underscores the holistic nature of health, highlighting the importance of addressing both physical and emotional aspects for a balanced and resilient life.

2.3 Meal Planning and Healthy Eating Habits

Meal planning and cultivating healthy eating habits are essential components of maintaining overall well-being and managing stress. By making thoughtful choices about what you eat and how you approach meals, you can support your physical health, boost your mood, and enhance your resilience. Here's a guide to effective meal planning and developing healthy eating habits:

1. Plan Ahead: Set aside time each week to plan your meals. Consider your schedule, dietary preferences, and nutritional goals.
Create a menu for the week, including breakfast, lunch, dinner, and snacks. This helps you avoid making impulsive, less healthy choices.

2. Balanced Meals: Aim for balanced meals that include a variety of nutrients. Each meal should ideally include lean protein, whole grains, healthy fats, and plenty of fruits and vegetables.

3. Portion Control: Pay attention to portion sizes to avoid overeating. Use smaller plates, bowls, and utensils to help manage portions.

4. Whole Foods: Choose whole, unprocessed foods as the foundation of your diet. Fresh fruits, vegetables,

whole grains, lean proteins, and healthy fats provide
essential nutrients and promote overall health.

5. Mindful Eating: Eat slowly and mindfully, savoring
each bite. Pay attention to the flavors, textures, and
sensations of your food.
Avoid distractions like screens or work while eating.
Focus on the experience of eating to prevent overeating
and improve digestion.

6. Hydration: Drink plenty of water throughout the day.
Staying hydrated supports digestion, energy levels, and
overall well-being.

7. Snack Smartly: Choose nutrient-dense snacks like
fruits, vegetables, nuts, and yogurt. Avoid sugary and
processed snacks.

8. Limit Processed Foods: Minimize your intake of
highly processed foods that are often high in added
sugars, unhealthy fats, and additives.

9. Include Fiber: Foods rich in dietary fiber, such as
whole grains, legumes, fruits, and vegetables, promote
digestive health and help you feel full.

10. Variety and Color: Include a wide variety of foods
in your diet to ensure you get a range of nutrients. Aim
for a colorful plate with different fruits and vegetables.

11. Plan for Treats: It's okay to indulge in occasional treats, but do so mindfully and in moderation. Allow yourself to enjoy your favorite treats without guilt.

12. Listen to Your Body: Pay attention to your hunger and fullness cues. Eat when you're hungry, and stop when you're satisfied.

13. Cook at Home: Cooking meals at home gives you control over ingredients and preparation methods. It can also be a creative and rewarding experience.

14. Seek Professional Guidance: If you have specific dietary goals, health concerns, or restrictions, consider consulting a registered dietitian or nutritionist for personalized guidance.

Developing healthy eating habits and practicing mindful meal planning can contribute to better physical health, enhanced mood, and improved stress management. By nourishing your body with wholesome foods and adopting mindful eating practices, you build a foundation for overall well-being and resilience.

Chapter 3: Quality Rest: Prioritizing Sleep and Recovery

Quality rest is an essential pillar of well-being and stress management. It involves getting sufficient, restorative sleep and incorporating relaxation into your daily routine. Here are some brief thoughts on the importance of quality rest:

1. Sleep's Restorative Power: Adequate sleep supports physical and mental recovery, allowing your body to repair itself and your mind to process emotions and experiences.

2. Cognitive Function and Mood: Quality rest enhances cognitive functions like memory, focus, and problem-solving, contributing to improved decision-making and emotional well-being.

3. Stress Resilience: Restful sleep bolsters your ability to cope with stress and enhances your emotional resilience, making you better equipped to handle challenges.

4. Energy and Vitality: Quality rest replenishes your energy reserves, boosts your vitality, and enables you to approach each day with vigor.

5. Sleep Hygiene: Adopting good sleep hygiene practices, such as maintaining a consistent sleep schedule, creating a comfortable sleep environment, and minimizing electronic devices before bedtime, can contribute to better sleep quality.

6. Relaxation and Self-Care: Beyond nighttime sleep, incorporating relaxation techniques like meditation, deep breathing, and mindful breaks throughout the day can further promote quality rest and stress relief.

7. Individual Needs: The amount of rest needed varies among individuals, but prioritizing both sleep and relaxation ensures that you're giving your body and mind the opportunity to rejuvenate.

8. Holistic Health: Quality rest is an integral part of a holistic approach to well-being. It complements other practices like nutrition, exercise, and stress management to create a balanced and resilient lifestyle.

Incorporating strategies to enhance your sleep quality and prioritize relaxation can have far-reaching benefits, positively influencing your mental, emotional, and physical health.

3.1 Understanding Sleep Cycles and Their Importance

Sleep cycles are recurring patterns of brain activity and physiological changes that occur during different stages of sleep. Understanding sleep cycles is crucial for comprehending the various stages of sleep and how they contribute to overall health, cognitive function, and emotional well-being. Here's an overview of sleep cycles and their importance:

1. Stages of Sleep:

a. Non-REM Sleep:

- **Stage 1**: This is a transitional stage between wakefulness and sleep, lasting a few minutes. Muscle activity decreases, and you may experience light, drifting sleep.

- **Stage 2**: A deeper sleep stage characterized by slower brain waves and occasional bursts of rapid brain activity (sleep spindles). Heart rate and body temperature decrease.

- **Stage 3**: Also known as slow-wave sleep (SWS), this is a deep and restorative sleep stage. It's important for physical restoration, immune function, and memory consolidation.

b. REM Sleep:
Rapid Eye Movement (REM) sleep is characterized by rapid eye movements, increased brain activity, and vivid dreaming. REM sleep is crucial for cognitive processes like learning and memory consolidation.

2. Importance of Sleep Cycles:

- **Physical Restoration**: Slow-wave sleep (Stage 3) is associated with physical restoration, including cell repair, immune system enhancement, and the release of growth hormones.

- **Cognitive Function**: REM sleep is linked to cognitive processes, including memory consolidation, problem-solving, and creative thinking. Adequate REM sleep supports optimal brain function.

- **Emotional Well-Being**: Sleep cycles play a role in regulating mood and emotional processing. Insufficient REM sleep has been linked to emotional disturbances and mood disorders.

- **Energy Conservation**: Sleep cycles help conserve energy by reducing metabolic activity during non-REM sleep stages, allowing the body to recuperate and recharge.

- **Stress Management**: Proper sleep cycles contribute to stress management by allowing the body to recover from daily stressors and maintaining hormonal balance.

- **Learning and Memory**: leep cycles facilitate the consolidation of new information and experiences, aiding in the formation of long-term memories.

- **Hormonal Regulation**: Sleep cycles influence the release of hormones that regulate appetite, stress response, and overall physiological balance.

- **Overall Health**: Disruption of sleep cycles, such as irregular sleep patterns or sleep deprivation, has been linked to a higher risk of chronic health conditions, including cardiovascular diseases, diabetes, and obesity.

3. Creating Healthy Sleep Patterns:

- Prioritize consistent sleep schedules to support regular sleep cycles.

- Create a comfortable sleep environment conducive to relaxation and rest.

- Limit exposure to electronic screens before bedtime to help regulate the body's natural sleep-wake cycle.

- Engage in relaxation techniques like deep breathing, meditation, or gentle stretches to promote better sleep quality.

- If sleep disturbances persist, consult a healthcare professional to address any underlying issues affecting your sleep cycles.

Understanding and respecting your body's natural sleep cycles can significantly impact your overall well-being, cognitive function, and emotional resilience. Prioritizing quality sleep contributes to a balanced and fulfilling lifestyle.

3.2 Creating a Relaxing Bedtime Routine

A relaxing bedtime routine is a series of calming activities you engage in before sleep to signal to your body and mind that it's time to wind down and prepare for rest. Establishing a consistent bedtime routine can improve sleep quality, help you fall asleep faster, and contribute to overall well-being. Here are some steps to creating an effective and relaxing bedtime routine:

1. Set a Consistent Schedule:
Try to go to bed and wake up at the same time every day, even on weekends. Consistency helps regulate your body's internal clock and improves sleep quality.

2. Limit Screen Time:
Dim the lights and reduce exposure to electronic screens (phones, tablets, and computers) at least an hour before bedtime. The blue light emitted by screens can interfere with the production of the sleep hormone melatonin.

3. Create a Calming Environment:
Make your bedroom conducive to relaxation and sleep. Keep the room cool, dark, and quiet. Consider using blackout curtains and white noise machines if needed.

4. Hygiene and Self-Care:
Take a warm bath or shower before bed. This can help
relax your muscles and promote a sense of calm.

5. Mindful Activities:
Engage in activities that promote relaxation, such as
reading a book (preferably a physical book instead of a
screen), practicing gentle stretching, or doing deep
breathing exercises.

6. Herbal Teas:
Sip on caffeine-free herbal teas like chamomile,
lavender, or valerian root, which have calming properties
and can help you unwind.

7. Progressive Muscle Relaxation:
Practice progressive muscle relaxation by consciously
tensing and then releasing different muscle groups in
your body. This can alleviate physical tension and
promote relaxation.

8. Mindfulness Meditation:
Engage in a short mindfulness meditation session. Focus
on your breath and let go of any racing thoughts.
Mindfulness can help quiet the mind and reduce stress.

9. Aromatherapy:
Use calming essential oils, such as lavender or bergamot,
in a diffuser or as a part of a nighttime skincare routine
to create a soothing atmosphere.

10. Limit Heavy Meals and Caffeine:
Avoid heavy meals and caffeine close to bedtime, as
they can disrupt sleep. Opt for light, easily digestible
snacks if you're hungry before bed.

11. Write in a Journal:
Spend a few minutes jotting down your thoughts,
worries, or things you're grateful for. This can help clear
your mind and promote a sense of closure before sleep.

12. Avoid Stressful Activities:
Try to avoid work-related tasks, intense discussions, or
engaging in emotionally charged activities close to
bedtime.

Creating a relaxing bedtime routine helps shift your
focus away from the stresses of the day and prepares you
for a peaceful night's sleep. Experiment with different
activities and find a routine that resonates with you and
helps you unwind. Consistently practicing these calming
activities can signal to your body that it's time to relax
and encourage a more restful night's sleep.

3.3 Addressing Insomnia and Sleep Disruptions

Insomnia and sleep disruptions can significantly impact
your well-being and daily functioning. If you're
struggling with sleep issues, it's important to address

them to improve your sleep quality and overall health. Here are some strategies to help you manage insomnia and sleep disruptions:

1. Identify the Causes:
Before addressing insomnia, it's important to identify any underlying causes. Common factors include stress, anxiety, depression, medical conditions, medications, caffeine, alcohol, and irregular sleep schedules.

2. **Establish a Sleep Schedule**:
Set a consistent sleep schedule by going to bed and waking up at the same time every day, even on weekends. This helps regulate your body's internal clock.

3. Create a Relaxing Bedtime Routine:
Develop a calming bedtime routine that includes activities like reading, gentle stretching, meditation, or deep breathing. This signals to your body that it's time to wind down.

4. Manage Stress and Anxiety:
Practice stress-reduction techniques, such as mindfulness, meditation, progressive muscle relaxation, and journaling, to help alleviate anxiety and promote relaxation.

5. Limit Screen Time:
Minimize exposure to screens (phones, tablets, and computers) at least an hour before bedtime, as the blue light can interfere with melatonin production.

6. Create a Comfortable Sleep Environment:
Ensure your bedroom is conducive to sleep by keeping it
dark, quiet, and at a comfortable temperature. Consider
using earplugs, eye shades, or white noise machines if
needed.

7. Be Mindful of Diet:
Avoid heavy meals, caffeine, and alcohol close to
bedtime, as they can disrupt sleep. Opt for light, easily
digestible snacks if needed.

8. Get Regular Physical Activity:
Engage in regular exercise, but try to finish intense
workouts at least a few hours before bedtime, as they can
be stimulating.

9. Manage Naps:
If you need to nap during the day, keep it short (20–30
minutes) and earlier in the day to avoid interfering with
nighttime sleep.

**10. Cognitive Behavioral Therapy for Insomnia
(CBT-I)**:
CBT-I is a structured program that addresses the
underlying thoughts, behaviors, and habits contributing
to insomnia. It's considered an effective approach for
managing sleep issues.

11. Consult a Healthcare Professional:
If your sleep disruptions persist or worsen, consider
seeking guidance from a healthcare provider. They can

help identify any underlying medical conditions and recommend appropriate treatments.

12. Avoid Clock-Watching:
If you're having trouble falling asleep, avoid constantly checking the clock, as it can increase anxiety about not sleeping.

Addressing insomnia and sleep disruptions often involves a combination of lifestyle adjustments, behavioral changes, and sometimes medical intervention. By implementing these strategies and creating healthy sleep habits, you can improve your sleep quality and restore a more consistent and restful sleep pattern.

Chapter 4: Stress-Busting Strategies: Effective Coping Techniques

Stress is a natural part of life, but chronic or excessive stress can take a toll on your well-being. Practicing effective stress-busting strategies can help you manage and reduce stress, promoting a healthier and more balanced life. Here are some strategies to help you bust stress:

1. Mindfulness and Meditation:
Mindfulness involves staying present and aware of your thoughts and sensations without judgment. Meditation practices, such as deep breathing, guided meditation, and body scanning, can help you relax and refocus your mind.

2. Physical Activity:
Regular exercise releases endorphins, which are natural stress-relievers. Engaging in physical activities you enjoy, such as walking, yoga, swimming, or dancing, can help reduce stress and improve your mood.

3. Deep Breathing Exercises:
Deep breathing techniques, like diaphragmatic breathing or box breathing, can activate the body's relaxation response and help reduce stress.

4. Progressive Muscle Relaxation:
This technique involves systematically tensing and relaxing different muscle groups, promoting physical relaxation and alleviating tension.

5. Journaling:
Writing down your thoughts, feelings, and worries can provide a sense of catharsis and help you gain perspective on your stressors.

6. Social Support:
Connecting with friends, family, or support groups can provide a sense of belonging and emotional relief. Sharing your feelings with others can help lighten your mental load.

7. Time Management:
Organize your tasks and prioritize them based on their importance. Break larger tasks into smaller, manageable steps to reduce overwhelm.

8. Healthy Eating:
A balanced diet rich in nutrients supports your body's ability to manage stress. Avoid excessive caffeine and sugar, as they can contribute to anxiety and mood swings.

9. Adequate Sleep:

Prioritize quality sleep by establishing a consistent sleep schedule and creating a relaxing bedtime routine.

10. Laughter and Humor:
Engaging in activities that make you laugh can trigger the release of endorphins and promote a sense of joy and relaxation.

11. Creative Outlets:
Expressing yourself through art, music, writing, or other creative activities can serve as a productive and enjoyable way to manage stress.

12. Set Boundaries:
Learn to say no when necessary and establish healthy boundaries to prevent overcommitting and burnout.

13. Nature and Fresh Air:
Spending time in nature or simply getting some fresh air can have a rejuvenating effect and help clear your mind.

14. Professional Support:
If stress becomes overwhelming, seeking guidance from a mental health professional, counselor, or therapist can provide you with effective coping strategies and support.

Remember that everyone is unique, so it's important to explore and experiment with different stress-busting strategies to find what works best for you. Combining these techniques and making them a part of your daily routine can help you manage stress and cultivate a more resilient and balanced life.

4.1 Deep Breathing and Relaxation Exercises

Deep breathing and relaxation exercises are powerful tools for managing stress and promoting a sense of calm and well-being. These techniques engage the body's relaxation response, helping to reduce the physiological effects of stress and anxiety. Here's more information on how deep breathing and relaxation exercises can help you cope with stress:

1. Deep Breathing Techniques:

a. Diaphragmatic Breathing (Belly Breathing):

- Inhale deeply through your nose, allowing your abdomen to rise as you fill your lungs.

- Exhale slowly through your mouth, feeling your abdomen lower.

- Focus on the rise and fall of your belly, rather than shallow chest breathing.

- Repeat for several breaths, gradually increasing the duration.

b. Box Breathing:

- Inhale deeply for a count of four.

- Hold your breath for a count of four.

- Exhale slowly for a count of four.

- Pause and hold for a count of four before inhaling again.

- Continue this pattern for several cycles.

2. Relaxation Exercises:

a. Progressive Muscle Relaxation:

- Tense and then relax different muscle groups in your body, starting from your toes and working your way up to your head.

- Focus on the sensation of relaxation as you release tension in each muscle group.

b. Guided Imagery:

- Close your eyes and imagine a peaceful and calming scene, such as a beach, forest, or meadow.

- Engage your senses by visualizing details, like the sound of waves or the scent of flowers.

c. Body Scan Meditation:

- Lie down or sit comfortably and bring your attention to different parts of your body, starting from your toes and moving upward.

- Notice any areas of tension or discomfort, and consciously release them as you breathe deeply.

d. Mindfulness Meditation:

- Sit or lie down in a comfortable position.

- Focus your attention on your breath, observing each inhalation and exhalation without judgment.

- When your mind wanders, gently bring your focus back to your breath.

e. Autogenic Relaxation:

- Mentally repeat a series of phrases that focus on feelings of warmth and heaviness in different parts of your body.

- This technique promotes a sense of relaxation and well-being.

Benefits of Deep Breathing and Relaxation Exercises:

- **Reduced Stress Hormones**: Deep breathing and relaxation exercises activate the parasympathetic nervous system, which helps lower stress hormone levels.

- **Lower Heart Rate and Blood Pressure**: These techniques can lead to a slower heart rate and reduced blood pressure, promoting a sense of calm.

- **Improved Focus and Clarity**: Relaxation exercises can clear your mind, improve concentration, and enhance cognitive function.

- **Enhanced Mood**: Deep breathing and relaxation promote the release of endorphins, which are natural mood boosters.

- **Better Sleep**: Practicing relaxation techniques before bed can help improve sleep quality and promote a restful night's sleep.

Incorporating deep breathing and relaxation exercises into your daily routine, especially during times of stress, can have a profound impact on your overall well-being. Consistent practice can help you manage stress more effectively and cultivate a greater sense of peace and resilience.

4.2 Progressive Muscle Relaxation

Progressive Muscle Relaxation (PMR) is a relaxation technique that involves systematically tensing and then relaxing different muscle groups in your body. This method helps release physical tension and promotes a sense of relaxation, making it an effective way to cope with stress and reduce anxiety. Here's how PMR works and how you can use it to manage stress:

1. How Progressive Muscle Relaxation Works:

- **Awareness**: Begin by finding a quiet and comfortable place to sit or lie down. Close your eyes and take a few deep breaths to settle into the present moment.

- **Tensing Phase**: Start with a specific muscle group, typically beginning with your toes or feet. Tense the muscles in that area as tightly as you can, holding the tension for about 5–10 seconds. Focus on the sensation of tension.

- **Relaxation Phase**: Suddenly release the tension and let the muscles completely relax. Notice the difference between the feeling of tension and relaxation. Focus on the sensation of relief and relaxation in that muscle group.

- **Progression**: Move systematically through your body, working your way up from your feet to your head. Focus on each muscle group individually, repeating the process of tensing and relaxing.

- **Breathing**: Throughout the exercise, maintain slow and deep breaths. Inhale as you tense the muscles, and exhale as you release them.

Benefits of Progressive Muscle Relaxation:

- **Physical Relaxation**: PMR helps release muscle tension, reducing physical discomfort and promoting a sense of physical calmness.

- **Stress Reduction**: By focusing on the physical sensations of relaxation, PMR distracts your mind from stressors and anxious thoughts.

- **Mind-Body Connection**: PMR enhances your awareness of how tension and relaxation feel in different muscle groups, promoting mindfulness.

- **Improved Sleep**: Practicing PMR before bedtime can help relax your body and mind, leading to better sleep quality.

- **Lowered Anxiety**: Regular practice of PMR can reduce overall anxiety levels and help you manage stress more effectively.

2. How to Practice Progressive Muscle Relaxation:

- **Learn the Technique**: Familiarize yourself with the steps of PMR and the muscle groups you'll be focusing on.

- **Set Aside Time**: Dedicate 10–15 minutes to practicing PMR in a quiet and comfortable environment.

- **Consistent Practice**: Regular practice is key. Aim to practice PMR daily or whenever you're feeling stressed or tense.

- **Adapt to Your Needs**: Modify the technique to fit your preferences. You can focus on fewer muscle groups or combine PMR with deep breathing and visualization.

- **Guided Sessions**: You can find guided PMR sessions online or in relaxation apps to help you follow along.

Progressive Muscle Relaxation is a simple yet effective technique that you can incorporate into your stress management toolkit. With practice, PMR can help you cultivate a greater sense of relaxation, reduce physical tension, and better cope with the demands of daily life.

4.3 Guided Imagery and Visualization

Imagery and visualization are powerful mental techniques that involve creating vivid and detailed mental images or scenes. These techniques can be used as effective stress coping strategies to promote relaxation, reduce anxiety, and enhance overall well-being. Here's how imagery and visualization work and how you can use them to manage stress:

1. How Imagery and Visualization Work:

Imagery and visualization leverage the mind's ability to create and experience sensory-rich mental scenarios. By engaging your senses and emotions in a positive and calming way, you can shift your focus away from stressors and induce a state of relaxation.

2. Using Imagery and Visualization For Stress Coping:

- **Select a Relaxing Scenario**: Choose a calming and pleasant mental scenario to visualize. This could be a serene beach, a tranquil forest, a peaceful garden, or any place where you feel safe and at ease.

- **Set the Scene**: Close your eyes and imagine yourself in your chosen setting. Engage your senses by focusing on the sights, sounds, smells, and sensations of the environment.

- **Detail and Vividness**: Make the mental image as vivid as possible. Imagine the colors, textures, and details of your surroundings. Immerse yourself in the experience.

- **Engage Emotions**: Connect with the positive emotions associated with your chosen scene. Feel the calmness, serenity, and relaxation that the scenario brings.

- **Stay Present**: If your mind starts to wander, gently bring your focus back to the visualization. You can use phrases like "I am calm" or "I am safe" to anchor your thoughts.

- **Practice Regularly**: Dedicate a few minutes each day to practicing imagery and visualization. It's especially effective when combined with deep breathing or progressive muscle relaxation.

Benefits of Imagery and Visualization For Stress Coping:

- **Relaxation Response**: Imagery and visualization activate the relaxation response, which reduces stress hormones and promotes a sense of calm.

- **Positive Focus**: By directing your attention to a pleasant mental scene, you shift your focus away from stressors and negative thoughts.

- **Mind-Body Connection**: Visualization enhances the mind-body connection, allowing you to tap into your body's natural ability to influence emotions and stress responses.

- **Anxiety Reduction**: Regular practice of imagery and visualization can help lower anxiety levels and promote emotional well-being.

- **Enhanced Resilience**: Engaging in positive mental imagery can help you build resilience by cultivating a sense of inner calm and resourcefulness.

3. Tips for Effective Imagery and Visualization:

- Start with simple scenarios and gradually add details as you become more comfortable.
- Customize the visualization to your preferences. Your calming scene can be as unique as you are.

- Use guided imagery recordings or scripts if you prefer structured guidance.

- Experiment with different settings and scenarios to find what resonates best with you.

- Imagery and visualization are versatile tools that can be used virtually anywhere, making them valuable assets in your stress management toolkit. By incorporating these techniques into your routine, you can create moments of relaxation, reduce stress, and cultivate a greater sense of well-being.

Chapter 5: Time Management And Productivity: Finding Balance

Effective time management and productivity strategies play a significant role in managing stress and promoting a balanced and fulfilling life. By managing your time more efficiently, you can reduce overwhelm, increase your sense of control, and create space for relaxation and self-care. Here's how time management and productivity contribute to stress management:

1. Prioritize Tasks:
Identify your most important tasks and prioritize them based on their significance and deadlines. Focus on completing high-priority tasks first.

2. Set Clear Goals:
Define clear and achievable goals for the day, week, or month. Having a sense of purpose and direction helps you stay focused and motivated.

3. Break Tasks Down:
Divide larger tasks into smaller, manageable steps. This approach makes tasks feel less daunting and allows you to make steady progress.

4. Use Time Blocks:
Allocate specific time blocks for different tasks or activities. Work on a task for a set period, then take a short break before moving on to the next task.

5. Avoid Multitasking:
Focus on one task at a time to increase efficiency and reduce mental strain. Multitasking can lead to decreased productivity and increased stress.

6. Practice the Two-Minute Rule:
If a task takes two minutes or less to complete, do it immediately. This prevents small tasks from piling up and causing stress.

7. Limit Distractions:

Minimize distractions by silencing notifications, closing unnecessary tabs, and creating a dedicated workspace. Distractions can disrupt your flow and increase stress.

8. Learn to Say No:
Recognize your limits and avoid overcommitting. Politely decline tasks or requests that do not align with your priorities.

9. Delegate and Collaborate:
Delegate tasks when possible, and collaborate with others to share the workload. Effective teamwork can help reduce stress and improve outcomes.

10. Take Breaks:
Regular breaks, even short ones, help refresh your mind and prevent burnout. Use breaks to stretch, move, or engage in a brief relaxation activity.

11. Use Productivity Techniques:
Explore productivity techniques like the Pomodoro Technique (work in focused intervals followed by short breaks) or the Eisenhower Matrix (prioritize tasks based on urgency and importance).

12. Reflect and Adjust:
Regularly assess your time management strategies to identify what's working and what needs adjustment. Flexibility is key to optimizing your approach.

Benefits of Effective Time Management for Stress Management:

- **Reduced Overwhelm**: Efficiently managing your tasks and schedule can reduce the feeling of being overwhelmed by responsibilities.

- **Increased Control**: Taking charge of your time allows you to feel more in control of your day and reduces stress.

- **Enhanced Focus**: By allocating dedicated time for tasks, you can focus more deeply, complete tasks more efficiently, and reduce stress caused by procrastination.

- **Time for Self-Care**: Effective time management creates room for self-care activities such as exercise, relaxation, and spending time with loved ones.

- **Improved Work-Life Balance**: Balancing work and personal lives helps prevent burnout and contributes to overall well-being.

Implementing time management and productivity strategies can lead to a more organized, balanced, and less stressful life. While it may take some trial and error to find the techniques that work best for you, the benefits of reduced stress and increased productivity are well worth the effort.

5.1 Setting Priorities and Managing Overwhelm

Setting priorities and managing overwhelm are essential skills for maintaining balance, productivity, and well-being in a fast-paced world. When you effectively prioritize tasks and cope with overwhelm, you can reduce stress and work towards your goals more efficiently. Here's a deeper look at setting priorities and strategies for managing overwhelm:

1. Setting Priorities:

- **Identify Goals**: Clarify your short-term and long-term goals. Knowing what you want to achieve helps you allocate your time and resources effectively.

- **Categorize Tasks**: Divide tasks into categories like "urgent," "important," and "not urgent or important." This helps you focus on what truly matters.

- **Use the Eisenhower Matrix**: Prioritize tasks based on their urgency and importance using the four quadrants of the matrix: Do First, Schedule, Delegate, and Eliminate.

- **Consider Impact**: Evaluate the potential impact of each task. Focus on tasks that contribute significantly to your goals or have high consequences.

- **Time-Blocking**: Allocate specific time blocks for different types of tasks. This helps you manage your time and maintain focus.

2. Managing Overwhelm:

- **Break Tasks Down**: Divide larger tasks into smaller, manageable steps. Tackling smaller chunks reduces feelings of overwhelm.

- **Focus on One Thing**: Multitasking can lead to overwhelm. Prioritize one task at a time to maintain clarity and effectiveness.

- **Set Realistic Expectations**: Avoid over committing and setting unrealistic expectations for yourself. Be honest about what you can realistically achieve.

- **Practice Self-Care**: Make time for self-care activities like exercise, meditation, and spending time with loved ones. Self-care helps recharge your energy and resilience.

- **Use a To-Do List**: Create a to-do list to keep track of tasks. Crossing off completed items provides a sense of accomplishment and reduces overwhelm.

- **Learn to Delegate**: Don't hesitate to delegate tasks to others if possible. Sharing the workload can alleviate stress.

- **Limit Decision Fatigue**: Minimize decision-making overwhelm by establishing routines, automating tasks, and making decisions in advance.

- **Set Boundaries**: Say no when necessary to prevent overextending yourself. Establish boundaries to protect your time and well-being.

- **Practice Mindfulness**: Mindfulness techniques, such as deep breathing and meditation, can help you stay present and manage stress.

- **Support**: Reach out to colleagues, friends, or mentors for guidance and support when you're feeling overwhelmed.

Benefits of Effective Prioritization and Overwhelm Management:

- **Reduced Stress**: By focusing on high-priority tasks and managing overwhelm, you can reduce stress and anxiety.

- **Increased Productivity**: Prioritizing tasks and managing overwhelm enhances your efficiency and productivity.

- **Improved Decision-Making**: Setting priorities allows you to make informed decisions and allocate your resources wisely.

- **Enhanced Well-Being**: Managing overwhelm promotes a healthier work-life balance, contributing to overall well-being.

- **Greater Satisfaction**: Successfully accomplishing tasks and managing stress provides a sense of accomplishment and satisfaction.

By mastering the art of setting priorities and managing overwhelm, you can create a more balanced and fulfilling life, achieve your goals, and maintain a healthier relationship with work and daily responsibilities.

5.2 Techniques for Efficient Task Management

Efficient task management is crucial for productivity, stress reduction, and achieving your goals. Implementing effective techniques can help you stay organized, focused, and on track. Here are some techniques to optimize your task management:

1. To-Do Lists:
Create a daily or weekly to-do list outlining tasks and prioritize them. Checking off completed tasks provides a sense of accomplishment.

2. Prioritization:
Use techniques like the Eisenhower Matrix or the ABCD method to categorize tasks based on urgency and importance. Focus on high-priority items.

3. Time Blocking:
Allocate specific time blocks for tasks on your calendar. This helps you dedicate focused time to each task and prevents over committing.

4. Pomodoro Technique:
Work for a focused 25-minute period (a "Pomodoro"), followed by a 5-minute break. After four Pomodoros, take a longer break.

5. Eat That Frog:
Start your day by tackling your most challenging or important task (the "frog"). Once completed, you'll feel a sense of accomplishment.

6. Two-Minute Rule:
If a task takes two minutes or less, do it immediately rather than adding it to your to-do list.

7. Task Batching:
Group similar tasks together and complete them in a single session. This minimizes context switching and boosts efficiency.

8. Delegate:

Identify tasks that can be outsourced or assigned to others. Delegating frees up your time for more important responsibilities.

9. Kanban Boards:
Use physical or digital boards with columns like "To Do," "In Progress," and "Completed" to visualize and track task progress.

10. GTD (Getting Things Done):
Follow the GTD method by capturing all tasks in an inbox, clarifying their meaning and importance, organizing them into categories, prioritizing them, and reviewing them regularly.

11. Digital Task Managers:
Use task management apps like Todoist, Trello, Asana, or Notion to organize tasks, set deadlines, and collaborate with others.

12. Weekly Reviews:
Dedicate time each week to reviewing your tasks, adjusting priorities, and planning for the upcoming week.

13. Mind Mapping:
Create visual mind maps to brainstorm ideas, organize thoughts, and outline tasks and projects.

14. SMART Goals:
Set Specific, Measurable, Achievable, Relevant, and Time-bound goals for tasks and projects.

15. Automation and Templates:
Automate repetitive tasks or create templates for common activities to save time.

Benefits of Efficient Task Management:

- **Increased Productivity**: Efficient task management helps you accomplish more in less time.

- **Reduced Stress**: Organized tasks and clear priorities minimize stress and overwhelm.

- **Enhanced Focus**: Techniques like time blocking and the Pomodoro Technique improve focus and concentration.

- **Improved Decision-Making**: Prioritizing tasks helps you make informed decisions about where to allocate your resources.

- **Better Work-Life Balance**: Efficient task management leaves room for leisure, relaxation, and self-care.

Choosing and combining these techniques based on your preferences and work style can significantly improve your ability to manage tasks effectively, maintain productivity, and lead a more balanced life.

5.3 The Art of Saying No: Boundaries and Work-Life Balance

Saying no is a valuable skill that allows you to set boundaries, prioritize your commitments, and maintain your well-being. Learning how to say no effectively is essential for managing your time, energy, and resources, and it can greatly contribute to reducing stress and avoiding burnout. Here's how to master the art of saying no:

1. Understand Your Limits: Reflect on your capacity and what you can realistically take on without overextending yourself. Recognize that saying no is a way of respecting your limits.

2. Prioritize Your Commitments: Identify your core responsibilities, goals, and values. When you have a clear sense of your priorities, it's easier to say no to requests that don't align with them.

3. Be Assertive, Not Apologetic: When declining a request, communicate your decision confidently and assertively. You don't need to apologize for prioritizing your well-being.

4. Offer Alternatives: If you genuinely want to help but can't commit, suggest alternative solutions or offer assistance in a way that aligns with your availability.

5. Use "I" Statements: Express your decision using "I" statements to avoid sounding accusatory or confrontational. For example, "I'm currently focusing on another project" instead of "You're asking too much."

6. Be Honest and Transparent: Honesty is key. Explain your reasons for declining honestly and respectfully, even if it's simply because you need time for yourself.

7. Practice Empathy and Kindness: It's possible to say no while still being empathetic and kind. Acknowledge the request, express appreciation, and explain your decision without being dismissive.

8. Buy Time: If you're unsure, don't hesitate to ask for time to consider the request. This gives you the opportunity to evaluate your commitments and make an informed decision.

9. Use a Delayed Response: If you're uncomfortable saying no directly, you can use email or messaging to respond later, after you've had time to think.

10. It's Okay to Decline Politely: You don't owe a lengthy explanation for saying no. A simple, polite decline is sufficient.

11. Practice Saying No: Saying no is a skill that improves with practice. Start with smaller requests to build confidence.

12. Stay Firm: Be consistent in your decisions. If you say no, stick to your decision and avoid feeling guilty.

Benefits of Saying No:

- **Reduced Stress**: By declining commitments that don't align with your priorities, you reduce overwhelm and stress.

- **Maintained Well-Being**: Saying no helps you protect your time and energy, allowing you to take care of your physical and mental well-being.

- **Respected Boundaries**: Setting boundaries fosters respect for your time and limits from others.

- **Enhanced Focus**: By avoiding overcommitment, you can focus on tasks and activities that truly matter.

- **Improved Relationships**: Saying no authentically and respectfully contributes to healthier communication and more genuine relationships.

Remember that saying no is a healthy and necessary part of self-care. It allows you to make room for what truly matters and prevents burnout, contributing to a more balanced and fulfilling life.

Chapter 6: Effective Communication: Enhancing Relationships And Reducing Conflict

Effective communication is a powerful tool for managing stress, resolving conflicts, and maintaining healthy relationships. Clear and open communication can help you express your needs, set boundaries, and navigate challenging situations, ultimately reducing stress and promoting a more harmonious and supportive environment. Here's how effective communication is related to managing stress:

1. Expressing Needs:

Communicating your needs, concerns, and feelings allows others to understand your perspective and offer support. Bottling up emotions can lead to increased stress.

2. Setting Boundaries:
Clearly communicating your boundaries helps you manage your time and energy effectively, preventing overwhelm and burnout.

3. Resolving Conflicts:
Addressing conflicts openly and respectfully can prevent misunderstandings and alleviate the emotional toll that unresolved issues can have on your stress levels.

4. Seeking Help:
Communicating your challenges and seeking help from friends, family, or professionals can provide you with valuable support and coping strategies.

5. Active Listening:
Actively listening to others and understanding their perspectives fosters empathy and helps build strong relationships, reducing potential sources of stress.

6. Clarifying Expectations:
Clearly communicating expectations in personal and professional settings helps avoid misunderstandings and unnecessary stress.

7. Saying No:

Expressing your limitations and respectfully declining tasks or commitments you cannot manage helps you avoid overextension and stress.

8. Providing Feedback:
Offering constructive feedback and receiving it gracefully can lead to improved communication and enhanced teamwork, reducing tension and stress.

9. Mindful Communication:
Practicing mindfulness while communicating helps you stay present, avoid reacting impulsively, and engage in more thoughtful conversations.

10. Avoiding Assumptions:
Clarifying information and avoiding assumptions can prevent unnecessary stress caused by misunderstandings or misinterpretations.

Benefits of Effective Communication For Stress Management:

- **Reduced Misunderstandings**: Clear communication minimizes the chances of misunderstandings that can lead to stress.
- **Enhanced Support**: Effective communication allows you to reach out for help and receive the support you need during challenging times.

- **Improved Relationships**: Open and respectful communication fosters healthier relationships, which contribute to emotional well-being.

- **Conflict Resolution**: Addressing conflicts through effective communication helps reduce tension and emotional distress.

- **Increased Self-Awareness**: Engaging in open conversations encourages self-reflection and self-awareness, enabling you to manage stress proactively.

- **Strengthened Coping Skills**: Sharing your thoughts and emotions helps you process stress and develop effective coping strategies.

Incorporating effective communication techniques into your interactions can lead to a more harmonious and supportive environment, ultimately contributing to your overall stress management efforts.

6.1 Active Listening and Empathetic Communication

Active listening and empathetic communication are essential skills that facilitate meaningful and effective interactions with others. These skills not only enhance your relationships but also play a significant role in managing stress, resolving conflicts, and creating a supportive environment. Here's a closer look at active listening and empathetic communication:

1. Active Listening:

Active listening involves fully concentrating, understanding, responding, and remembering what is being said during a conversation. It goes beyond simply hearing words; it requires engaging with the speaker's thoughts, emotions, and intentions.

Key Elements of Active Listening:

- **Focus**: Give your full attention to the speaker. Put aside distractions and show genuine interest.

- **Nonverbal Cues**: Use appropriate nonverbal cues like eye contact, nodding, and facial expressions to convey that you're actively engaged.

- **Minimal Interruptions**: Allow the speaker to finish their thoughts before responding. Avoid interrupting or finishing their sentences.

- **Clarification**: Ask open-ended questions or paraphrase to ensure you've understood correctly.

- **Empathy**: Put yourself in the speaker's shoes and try to understand their feelings and perspective.

2. Empathetic Communication:

Empathetic communication involves not only understanding what someone is saying but also connecting with their emotions and demonstrating genuine concern for their well-being. It's about creating a safe space for the speaker to share their thoughts and feelings.

Key Elements of Empathetic Communication:

- **Active Listening**: Empathy begins with actively listening to the speaker's words and emotions.

- **Validation**: Acknowledge the speaker's feelings and experiences without judgment. Show that their emotions are valid and understood.

- **Reflecting Emotions**: Reflect back the speaker's emotions, showing that you understand and empathize with how they feel.

- **Offering Support**: Express your willingness to provide support, whether through words of encouragement, practical help, or simply being present.

- **Being Present**: Engage fully in the conversation without distraction. Show that you value the speaker's thoughts and feelings.

Benefits of Active Listening and Empathetic Communication For Stress Management:

- **Reduced Isolation**: Knowing that someone is truly listening and understanding can alleviate feelings of loneliness and isolation, reducing stress.

- **Conflict Resolution**: Active listening and empathy can defuse conflicts and create a more harmonious environment.

- **Stronger Relationships**: Empathetic communication builds trust and rapport, leading to stronger, more supportive relationships.

- **Emotional Regulation**: When you practice empathy, you help others regulate their emotions, which can contribute to a calmer atmosphere.

- **Support Network**: Being an empathetic listener can encourage others to open up and seek your support, creating a valuable network for stress management.

By developing active listening and empathetic communication skills, you can foster deeper connections, navigate challenging situations with greater understanding, and contribute to a more empathetic and less stressful environment for yourself and those around you.

6.2 Conflict Resolution Skills

Conflict is a natural part of human interactions, and developing effective conflict resolution skills is essential for maintaining healthy relationships, reducing stress, and fostering a positive environment. Here are key strategies and techniques for handling conflicts in a constructive and productive manner:

1. Stay Calm:

Maintain your composure and emotional balance. Avoid reacting impulsively or aggressively.

2. Active Listening:
Give your full attention to the other person's perspective. Listen without interrupting, and try to understand their viewpoint.

3. Empathy:
Put yourself in the other person's shoes. Understand their feelings and concerns, even if you disagree.

4. Use "I" Statements:
Express your thoughts and feelings using "I" statements to avoid sounding accusatory. For example, say, "I feel upset when..." rather than "You always..."

5. Focus on the Issue, Not the Person:
Address the problem at hand rather than attacking the person. Separate the behavior from the individual.

6. Clarify Misunderstandings:
Seek clarification to ensure you understand each other's perspectives accurately. Miscommunications often contribute to conflicts.

7. Find Common Ground:
Identify shared interests or goals that can serve as a basis for finding solutions.

8. Brainstorm Solutions:
Collaboratively generate possible solutions and
alternatives. Be open to compromise.

9. Maintain Respect:
Treat each other with respect and dignity, even during
disagreements. Avoid insults, name-calling, and hostile
language.

10. Take Breaks If necessary:
If emotions are running high, take a break to cool off
before continuing the conversation.

11. Seek Mediation:
If a conflict is particularly challenging, consider
involving a neutral third party to facilitate the discussion.

12. Focus on The Future:
Shift the focus from blame and past actions to finding a
solution that benefits everyone moving forward.

13. Apologize and Forgive:
If you've made a mistake, offer a sincere apology. Be
willing to forgive and let go of grudges.

14. Learn and Grow:
Reflect on the conflict afterward to gain insights into
improving communication and preventing similar issues
in the future.

- **Reduced Tension**: Addressing conflicts directly and constructively helps reduce tension and emotional stress.

- **Enhanced Communication**: Conflict resolution skills improve your ability to communicate effectively and understand others.

- **Stronger Relationships**: Successfully resolving conflicts builds trust and strengthens relationships.

- **Productive Problem-Solving**: Learning to navigate conflicts results in more effective problem-solving and decision-making.

- **Improved Well-Being**: Handling conflicts positively contributes to your emotional well-being and overall stress management.

By honing your conflict resolution skills, you empower yourself to navigate challenging situations with grace, promote understanding, and create a more harmonious and less stressful environment for yourself and those around you.

6.3 Building Supportive Social Connections

Strong and supportive social connections are vital for overall well-being, stress management, and a fulfilling life. Having a network of friends, family, and colleagues who provide emotional support, companionship, and a sense of belonging can significantly reduce stress and enhance your resilience. Here's how to build and nurture these connections:

1. Maintain Active Relationships:
Regularly engage with friends, family members, and acquaintances. Reach out, stay in touch, and make time for social interactions.

2. Be a Good Listener:
Show genuine interest in others, actively listen, and provide a safe space for them to share their thoughts and feelings.

3. Share and Be Open:
Be willing to share your thoughts, experiences, and emotions with others. Vulnerability fosters deeper connections.

4. Join Social Groups:
Participate in clubs, hobby groups, sports teams, or online communities that align with your interests. These provide opportunities to meet like-minded individuals.

5. Volunteer:
Engage in volunteer activities to connect with others who share your values and contribute to causes you care about.

6. Attend Events:
Attend social gatherings, parties, workshops, and community events to expand your social circle.

7. Reconnect With Old Friends:
Reach out to people from your past whom you've lost touch with. Rekindling old connections can be rewarding.

8. Support Others:
Offer your help, assistance, and encouragement to others when they're in need. Acts of kindness strengthen relationships.

9. Cultivate Empathy:
Understand and empathize with others' feelings and experiences. This fosters deeper connections and emotional support.

10. Online Networking:

Utilize social media and online platforms to connect with friends, family, and like-minded individuals.

11. Organize Gatherings:
Plan get-togethers, dinners, or outings to bring people together and strengthen your social network.

12. Quality Over Quantity:
Focus on building a few meaningful and supportive relationships rather than trying to maintain a large number of superficial connections.

Benefits of Supportive Social Connections:

- **Emotional Support**: Friends and loved ones provide a network of emotional support during challenging times.

- **Stress Reduction**: Engaging with supportive people can help alleviate stress and provide a sense of comfort.

- **Enhanced Resilience**: Strong social connections contribute to greater resilience in the face of adversity.

- **Positive Influence**: Supportive relationships encourage healthy behaviors, positive thinking, and effective stress coping strategies.

- **Improved Well-Being**: Meaningful social connections are associated with increased happiness, lower rates of anxiety and depression, and overall well-being.

Prioritizing the development and nurturing of supportive social connections is a proactive way to create a buffer against stress, enhance your emotional health, and enrich your life with meaningful relationships.

Chapter 7: Mindset Shift: Cultivating Resilience and Positive Thinking

A mindset shift involves changing your perspective, beliefs, and attitudes to approach situations in a more positive and empowered way. Adopting a new mindset can significantly impact how you perceive and manage stress. Here are some key mindset shifts that can contribute to effective stress management:

1. Embrace Challenges:
Shift from seeing challenges as obstacles to opportunities for growth. Embracing challenges helps you build resilience and develop coping skills.

2. Focus on What You Can Control:
Instead of fixating on things beyond your control, focus your energy on actions and decisions you can influence.

3. Practice Self-Compassion:
Replace self-criticism with self-compassion. Treat yourself with kindness and understanding, especially during difficult times.

4. Reframe Negative Thoughts:

Challenge and reframe negative thoughts and self-limiting beliefs. Replace them with more positive and constructive perspectives.

5. Cultivate Gratitude:

Shift your focus from what you lack to what you have. Regularly practice gratitude to foster a more positive outlook.

6. Emphasize Solutions:

Transition from dwelling on problems to seeking solutions. A problem-solving mindset encourages proactive action.

7. Prioritize Well-Being:

Shift from valuing productivity above all else to prioritizing your physical, mental, and emotional well-being.

8. Practice Mindfulness:

Develop a present-focused mindset through mindfulness. Be aware of your thoughts and emotions without judgment.

9. Seek Learning:

Adopt a growth mindset, where you view challenges as opportunities to learn and improve, rather than as threats.

10. Build Resilience:

Shift from viewing stress as solely negative to seeing it as a chance to build resilience and develop coping strategies.

11. Accept Imperfection:
Move away from perfectionism and embrace the idea that mistakes are part of the learning process.

12. Foster Positivity:
Cultivate a positive attitude by seeking out positive experiences, surrounding yourself with supportive people, and focusing on the good.

13. Set Realistic Expectations:
Adjust your expectations to be more realistic and aligned with your capabilities and circumstances.

14. Practice Self-Care:
Change from neglecting self-care to consistently prioritizing activities that nurture your physical, mental, and emotional well-being.

15. Be Present:
Shift from ruminating about the past or worrying about the future to being fully present in the moment.

Benefits of a Positive Mindset Shift for Stress Management:

- **Improved Coping**: A positive mindset equips you with effective coping skills to manage stress and challenges.

- **Reduced Stress Impact**: Shifting your perspective can mitigate the impact of stress on your mental and physical health.

- **Enhanced Well-Being**: A positive mindset contributes to increased overall well-being and a greater sense of happiness and contentment.

- **Better Decision-Making**: Positive thinking enhances clarity and rational decision-making, even in stressful situations.

- **Resilience Building**: A positive mindset fosters resilience, allowing you to bounce back from setbacks more effectively.

By intentionally cultivating a mindset shift, you can transform your relationship with stress, approach challenges with greater confidence, and create a more balanced and fulfilling life.

7.1 The Role of Resilience in Stress Management

Resilience is the ability to adapt, bounce back, and effectively cope with challenges, adversity, and stress. It plays a crucial role in stress management, helping individuals navigate difficult situations, maintain emotional well-being, and thrive despite the pressures of modern life. Here's how resilience contributes to effective stress management:

1. Adapting to Change: Resilient individuals are better equipped to handle unexpected changes and uncertainties. They view challenges as opportunities for growth and adaptation rather than insurmountable obstacles.

2. Coping with Adversity: Resilience provides a toolkit of coping strategies that help individuals manage stress and adversity more effectively. These strategies may include problem-solving, seeking social support, and maintaining a positive mindset.

3. Emotional Regulation: Resilience enables individuals to regulate their emotions and manage emotional reactions to stressors. This prevents overwhelming emotional responses and promotes a more balanced state of mind.

4. Optimism and Positive Thinking: Resilient people tend to maintain an optimistic outlook, focusing on potential solutions rather than dwelling on problems. This positive mindset contributes to effective stress management.

5. Healthy Relationships: Resilience fosters the ability to build and maintain supportive social connections. Strong relationships provide a network of emotional support during times of stress.

6. Flexible Thinking: Resilient individuals exhibit flexible thinking, adapting their perspectives and attitudes to different situations. This adaptability helps them find creative solutions to challenges.

7. Mindfulness and Self-Awareness: Resilience is often linked to mindfulness and self-awareness. Being attuned to one's thoughts, emotions, and reactions allows for better stress recognition and management.

8. Problem-Solving Skills: Resilience enhances problem-solving abilities, enabling individuals to approach stressors with a constructive mindset and seek effective solutions.

9. Reduced Impact of Stress: Resilient people are better equipped to handle stressors without experiencing the same level of distress. Their ability to manage stress prevents it from becoming chronic and harmful.

10. Physical Well-Being: Resilience can positively impact physical health by reducing the physiological effects of stress on the body, such as lowered immune function and increased inflammation.

11. Long-Term Well-Being: Developing resilience contributes to long-term well-being by equipping individuals with the skills needed to navigate life's ups and downs while maintaining emotional equilibrium.

Benefits of Resilience in Stress Management:

- **Reduced Emotional Distress**: Resilience helps individuals manage emotional reactions and prevent excessive distress during challenging times.

- **Improved Coping**: Resilience provides a toolbox of effective coping strategies that allow for healthier responses to stressors.

- **Enhanced Adaptability**: Resilience fosters adaptability and the ability to pivot in the face of change or adversity.

- **Strengthened Relationships**: Resilient individuals are better equipped to build and

maintain supportive relationships, which
contribute to stress reduction.

- **Positive Mindset**: Resilience promotes a positive
  outlook and the belief that challenges can be
  overcome, even in stressful situations.

Developing resilience is an ongoing process that
involves building and refining skills over time. Through
self-awareness, coping strategies, and a positive mindset,
individuals can enhance their ability to manage stress,
navigate life's challenges, and thrive in the face of
adversity.

7.2 Cognitive Restructuring and Reframing

Cognitive restructuring and reframing are powerful
cognitive-behavioral techniques that help individuals
manage stress by changing the way they perceive and
interpret situations. These techniques involve
challenging and replacing negative thought patterns with
more realistic, balanced, and positive ones. By altering
your cognitive perspective, you can effectively reduce
stress, anxiety, and emotional distress. Here's how
cognitive restructuring and reframing work:

1. Cognitive Restructuring:

Cognitive restructuring involves identifying and modifying distorted or unhelpful thought patterns that contribute to stress. These distorted thoughts, often referred to as "cognitive distortions," can magnify stressors and lead to increased emotional distress.

a. Steps in Cognitive Restructuring:

- **Identify Negative Thoughts**: Become aware of negative or irrational thoughts that arise in response to stressors.

- **Challenge Negative Thoughts**: Analyze the accuracy and validity of these thoughts. Are they based on evidence? Are they overly negative or catastrophic?

- **Replace With Balanced Thoughts**: Replace negative thoughts with more balanced, rational, and evidence-based alternatives. Consider alternative explanations or perspectives.

- **Practice and Reinforce**: Continuously practice recognizing and challenging negative thoughts, reinforcing the new balanced thoughts.

2. Reframing:

Reframing involves shifting your perspective to view a situation in a different light. It's about looking for alternative interpretations that emphasize the positive aspects or offer a broader understanding of the situation.

a. Types of Reframing:

i. Positive Reframing: Focus on the positive aspects or potential opportunities within a challenging situation. For example, seeing a setback as a chance to learn and grow.

ii. Contextual Reframing: Consider the broader context or long-term perspective to minimize the immediate stress of a situation. This involves understanding that current difficulties may be temporary.

iii. Empowerment Reframing: Reinterpret the situation in a way that empowers you, highlighting your ability to take control and make positive choices.

Benefits of Cognitive Restructuring and Reframing:

- **Stress Reduction**: By changing negative thought patterns, you reduce the emotional distress and anxiety associated with stress.

- **Enhanced Coping**: Cognitive restructuring and reframing provide healthier ways to cope with challenging situations.

- **Improved Problem-Solving**: A more balanced perspective allows for clearer thinking and better decision-making under stress.

- **Resilience Building**: Developing the ability to reframe situations enhances your resilience and adaptability.

- **Positive Mindset**: These techniques foster a more positive outlook on life, even during difficult times.

- **Reduced Rumination**: Challenging negative thoughts prevents excessive rumination, which can contribute to stress and anxiety.

Cognitive restructuring and reframing require practice and self-awareness. Over time, these techniques become valuable tools for managing stress, promoting emotional well-being, and developing a more constructive and balanced cognitive perspective.

7.3 Cultivating Gratitude and Optimism

Cultivating gratitude and optimism are powerful practices that can significantly contribute to effective stress management, improved emotional well-being, and a more positive outlook on life. These practices involve focusing on the positive aspects of your experiences and developing a mindset that promotes resilience and happiness. Here's how to cultivate gratitude and optimism:

1. Cultivating Gratitude:

Gratitude involves recognizing and appreciating the positive aspects of your life, even in the midst of challenges. It shifts your focus away from what's lacking and directs it toward what you have to be thankful for.

Ways to Cultivate Gratitude:

- **Gratitude Journal**: Regularly write down things you're grateful for. This practice helps you acknowledge the positives in your life.

- **Morning or Evening Ritual**: Set aside time each day to reflect on the things you're thankful for, either in the morning to start your day positively or in the evening to end it on a grateful note.

- **Express Appreciation**: Tell loved ones or colleagues how much you appreciate them and their contributions. This strengthens relationships and spreads positivity.

- **Mindful Gratitude**: Practice being present in the moment and appreciating the simple pleasures of life, such as a beautiful sunset or a warm cup of tea.

- **Shift Perspective**: When facing challenges, look for the silver lining or lessons you can learn. This reframing encourages a more positive outlook.

2. Cultivating Optimism:

Optimism is the belief that positive outcomes are possible and that challenges can be overcome. It involves approaching situations with a hopeful and constructive mindset.

Ways to Cultivate Optimism:

- **Positive Self-Talk**: Replace negative self-talk with positive affirmations and statements that reinforce your belief in your abilities.

- **Focus on Solutions**: When facing problems, shift your focus from the problem itself to potential solutions and steps you can take to address it.

- **Challenge Negative Thoughts**: When negative thoughts arise, challenge them by seeking evidence to support a more positive perspective.

- **Visualize Success**: Imagine successful outcomes and visualize yourself overcoming challenges. This mental rehearsal fosters optimism.

- **Learn from Setbacks**: View setbacks as learning experiences rather than failures. Emphasize the progress and growth that can come from challenges.

Benefits of Cultivating Gratitude and Optimism:

- **Stress Reduction**: Gratitude and optimism help reduce stress by shifting your focus away from negativity and promoting a positive mindset.

- **Improved Emotional Well-Being**: Cultivating these practices enhances your overall emotional

well-being and contributes to a more balanced
and contented life.

- **Enhanced Resilience**: Gratitude and optimism
  build resilience by fostering a mindset that
  focuses on solutions and growth rather than
  obstacles.

- **Better Coping**: When facing stressors, a grateful
  and optimistic outlook equips you with healthier
  coping strategies.

- **Positive Relationships**: Grateful and optimistic
  individuals tend to attract positive relationships
  and contribute to a more uplifting environment.

Incorporating gratitude and optimism into your daily life
takes effort and practice, but the benefits are well worth
it. These practices can transform your mindset, help you
manage stress more effectively, and contribute to a
happier and more fulfilling life.

Chapter 8: Emotional Intelligence: Navigating Emotions And Building Resilience

Emotional intelligence (EI) refers to the ability to recognize, understand, manage, and effectively use your own emotions and those of others. It plays a significant role in stress management by helping you navigate emotions, build healthy relationships, and cope with challenges in a balanced and adaptive manner. Here's how emotional intelligence contributes to effective stress management:

1. Self-Awareness:
Recognizing your own emotions, triggers, and stress responses is the first step in managing stress. Self-awareness allows you to identify when you're stressed and take proactive steps to address it.

2. Self-Regulation:
Emotional intelligence helps you regulate and manage your emotions, preventing them from overwhelming you. This includes finding healthy ways to cope with stress, such as deep breathing, mindfulness, or relaxation techniques.

3. Empathy:
Understanding and empathizing with others' emotions can improve your relationships and reduce interpersonal conflicts that contribute to stress.

4. Social Skills:
Effective communication, active listening, and conflict resolution are all parts of emotional intelligence. Developing strong social skills enhances your ability to navigate stressful interactions and maintain healthy relationships.

5. Stress Recognition:
Emotional intelligence enables you to recognize signs of stress not only in yourself but also in others. This awareness can lead to timely interventions and support.

6. Adaptive Coping:
With emotional intelligence, you're better equipped to choose adaptive coping strategies that align with the specific emotional context of a stressful situation.

7. Resilience Building:
Developing emotional intelligence helps build resilience, allowing you to bounce back more effectively from stressors and setbacks.

8. Positive Outlook:
Emotional intelligence contributes to a more optimistic and balanced outlook, enabling you to approach challenges with a sense of control and optimism.

9. Self-Care:
Understanding your emotional needs and boundaries allows you to prioritize self-care and prevent burnout.

10. Mindful Decision-Making:
Emotional intelligence guides you to make decisions mindfully, considering both your emotions and their potential emotional impact on others.

Benefits of Emotional Intelligence in Stress Management:

- **Better Stress Coping**: Emotional intelligence equips you with effective strategies to cope with stress, preventing emotional overwhelm.

- **Improved Communication**: Strong communication skills reduce misunderstandings and conflicts that can lead to stress.

- **Healthy Relationships**: Emotional intelligence fosters understanding, empathy, and positive interactions, enhancing your support network.

- **Reduced Emotional Reactions**: Being emotionally intelligent allows you to respond to stressors in a more measured and thoughtful manner.

- **Enhanced Resilience**: Emotional intelligence contributes to building resilience, which helps you adapt and thrive during challenging times.

- **Positive Outlook**: Developing emotional intelligence promotes a positive mindset and fosters a sense of control over your emotional responses.

Cultivating emotional intelligence is an ongoing process that involves self-awareness, practice, and continuous learning. As you enhance your emotional intelligence, you'll find yourself better equipped to manage stress, build healthier relationships, and lead a more balanced and fulfilling life.

8.1 Recognizing and Managing Emotions Effectively

Recognizing and managing emotions effectively is a fundamental skill for stress management and overall well-being. It involves understanding your own emotions, identifying triggers, and employing strategies to navigate them in a healthy and constructive manner. Here's a step-by-step guide to recognizing and managing emotions effectively:

1. Self-Awareness:
Pay attention to your emotional state throughout the day. Notice changes in your mood, energy level, and overall feelings.

2. Label Emotions:
Practice putting words to your emotions. Identify whether you're feeling happy, sad, anxious, frustrated, or any other specific emotion.

3. Understand Triggers:

Reflect on situations, people, or events that trigger specific emotions. Understand what prompts your emotional responses.

4. Physiological Signs:
Pay attention to physical sensations that accompany emotions, such as a racing heart, tense muscles, or shallow breathing.

5. Mindfulness and Presence:
Practice mindfulness to stay present and fully experience your emotions without judgment.

6. Reflect on Beliefs:
Explore the beliefs or thoughts that contribute to your emotional reactions. Are there cognitive distortions at play?

7. Accept Emotions:
Allow yourself to feel the full range of emotions without judgment. Accept that emotions are a natural part of being human.

8. Healthy Expression:
Find healthy outlets to express your emotions, such as journaling, talking to a friend, or engaging in creative activities.

9. Stress Management Techniques:

Employ stress management techniques like deep breathing, progressive muscle relaxation, or meditation to regulate intense emotions.

10. Cognitive Restructuring:
Challenge and reframe negative thought patterns that contribute to overwhelming emotions.

11. Problem-Solving:
If the emotion is linked to a specific issue, engage in problem-solving to address the root cause.

12. Seek Support:
 If needed, reach out to a trusted friend, family member, or professional for emotional support and guidance.

13. Time and Space:
Sometimes, giving yourself time and space to process emotions before responding can prevent impulsive reactions.

14. Practice Self-Compassion:
Be kind and understanding toward yourself, especially during moments of emotional distress.

15. Reflect and Learn:
After managing an emotion, reflect on what worked and what you learned from the experience.

Benefits of Recognizing and Managing Emotions:

- **Emotional Regulation**: Recognizing and managing emotions prevents emotional overwhelm and helps you respond more effectively to stressors.

- **Reduced Stress**: Healthy emotional management leads to reduced stress and anxiety levels.

- **Improved Relationships**: Understanding and managing your emotions enhances your ability to communicate and connect with others.

- **Better Decision-Making**: Emotionally intelligent decision-making leads to more thoughtful and rational choices, even under stress.

- **Enhanced Well-Being**: Effectively managing emotions contributes to overall emotional well-being and a more balanced life.

By cultivating the skill of recognizing and managing emotions effectively, you empower yourself to navigate stressors with greater ease, maintain emotional equilibrium, and develop a more resilient and adaptable approach to life's challenges.

8.2 Strategies for Emotional Regulation

Emotional regulation involves the ability to manage and modulate your emotions in healthy and constructive ways. By practicing effective emotional regulation strategies, you can navigate stress, maintain emotional balance, and enhance your overall well-being. Here are some strategies to help you regulate your emotions:

1. Deep Breathing:
Engage in deep, diaphragmatic breathing to calm your nervous system and reduce feelings of anxiety or stress.

2. Mindfulness Meditation:
Practice mindfulness meditation to stay present and observe your emotions without judgment. This helps you respond rather than react to them.

3. Progressive Muscle Relaxation:
Tense and then release different muscle groups to release physical tension associated with heightened emotions.

4. Grounding Techniques:

Focus on your senses by describing what you see, hear, feel, taste, and smell. Grounding brings you back to the present moment.

5. Visualization:
Imagine a calming and peaceful scene to reduce stress and induce relaxation.

6. Journaling:
Write down your thoughts and emotions to gain insight, process feelings, and develop a better understanding of your experiences.

7. Self-Compassion:
Treat yourself with kindness and understanding, especially during times of emotional distress.

8. Limit Negative Self-Talk:
Challenge and reframe negative thoughts that contribute to heightened emotions.

9. Exercise and Physical Activity:
Engage in regular physical activity to release endorphins, which are natural mood enhancers.

10. Creative Expression:
Express your emotions through creative outlets like art, music, or writing.

11. Social Support:
Talk to a friend, family member, or therapist to share your feelings and receive validation and support.

12. Engage in Hobbies:
Participate in activities you enjoy to shift your focus away from intense emotions.

13. Distraction Techniques:
Engage in activities that divert your attention from negative emotions, such as reading, cooking, or gardening.

14. Time-Outs:
Take short breaks to cool off and gain perspective before responding to emotionally charged situations.

15. Cognitive Reframing:
Challenge and replace negative or distorted thoughts with more balanced and rational ones.

16. Identify Triggers:
 Recognize situations, people, or circumstances that trigger strong emotions, and develop strategies to manage them.

17. Sleep and Rest:
Ensure you're getting enough quality sleep, as a lack of sleep can exacerbate emotional reactivity.

18. Practice Gratitude:

Focus on what you're thankful for to shift your perspective and reduce negative emotions.

19. Mindful Breathing:
Pay attention to your breath and use it as an anchor to bring your focus back to the present moment.

20. Seek Professional Help:
If emotions are overwhelming or persistent, consider speaking to a mental health professional for guidance.

Benefits of Emotional Regulation:

- **Stress Reduction**: Effective emotional regulation helps you manage stress and anxiety more efficiently.

- **Enhanced Coping**: You'll develop healthier ways to cope with challenging emotions and situations.

- **Improved Relationships**: Emotional regulation leads to better communication and more positive interactions with others.

- **Positive Well-Being**: By managing your emotions, you contribute to improved emotional well-being and a more balanced life.

Practicing emotional regulation strategies empowers you to respond to stressors in a controlled and healthy manner, fostering emotional resilience and enhancing your overall quality of life.

8.3 Developing Empathy and Social Awareness

Empathy and social awareness are essential components of emotional intelligence that play a significant role in stress management and building positive relationships. Developing these skills allows you to connect with others on a deeper level, understand their perspectives, and navigate social interactions with greater understanding and compassion. Here's how to cultivate empathy and social awareness:

1. Active Listening:
Pay full attention when others are speaking, without interrupting or planning your response. This shows respect and fosters a deeper connection.

2. Put Yourself in Their Shoes:
Imagine how someone else might be feeling or what they might be experiencing in a given situation.

3. Ask Open-Ended Questions:
Encourage others to share their thoughts and feelings by asking open-ended questions that promote meaningful conversations.

4. Practice Non-Judgment:
Suspend judgment and refrain from jumping to conclusions about someone's feelings or experiences.

5. Observe Body Language:
Pay attention to nonverbal cues, such as facial expressions and posture, to gain insights into others' emotions.

6. Show Genuine Interest:
Demonstrate curiosity and interest in others' lives, experiences, and stories.

7. Validate Emotions:
Acknowledge and validate the emotions that others are experiencing, even if you don't necessarily agree with their viewpoint.

8. Cultivate Cultural Sensitivity:
Develop an understanding and appreciation for different cultural perspectives and practices.

9. Read Emotional Cues:
Become attuned to emotional cues in conversations and adjust your responses accordingly.

10. Reflect on Your Interactions:

After social interactions, take a moment to reflect on how you demonstrated empathy and consider how you can improve.

11. Practice Empathetic Responses:
Respond to others' emotions with empathy and support, rather than dismissing or minimizing their feelings.

12. Volunteer and Engage in Community Activities:
Participate in activities that bring you into contact with different people and allow you to understand various perspectives.

13. Learn About Others' Experiences:
Educate yourself about the experiences and challenges faced by individuals from different backgrounds.

14. Mindful Observation:
Observe the dynamics of social interactions around you, noticing how people express emotions and respond to each other.

15. Seek Feedback:
Ask for feedback from friends or colleagues about your ability to empathize and demonstrate social awareness.

Benefits of Developing Empathy and Social Awareness:

- **Enhanced Relationships**: Developing empathy strengthens your relationships by fostering understanding and connection.

- **Conflict Resolution**: Empathy helps you navigate conflicts more effectively by considering others' perspectives.

- **Reduced Stress**: Understanding others' emotions and needs can lead to smoother interactions and reduced stress.

- **Effective Communication**: Empathy improves communication by promoting active listening and the effective expression of emotions.

- **Cultural Competence**: Social awareness enhances your ability to navigate diverse social environments and understand different cultural contexts.

Cultivating empathy and social awareness is an ongoing process that involves self-reflection, practice, and continuous learning. These skills not only contribute to stress management but also enrich your interactions, promote positive relationships, and create a more empathetic and compassionate world.

Chapter 9: Hobbies, Passion, And Play: Finding Joy Amidst The Chaos

Engaging in hobbies, pursuing passions, and incorporating play into your life are essential components of effective stress management. These activities provide a healthy outlet for relaxation, self-expression, and enjoyment, helping you reduce stress, enhance your well-being, and maintain a balanced and fulfilling lifestyle. Here's how hobbies, passion, and play contribute to stress management:

1. Hobbies:

Hobbies are activities that you enjoy and engage in for leisure and pleasure. They provide a break from daily routines, allowing you to immerse yourself in something you're passionate about.

Benefits of Hobbies:

- **Stress Relief**: Hobbies offer an escape from stressors and help you recharge both mentally and emotionally.

- **Mindfulness**: Engaging in a hobby can promote mindfulness, where you focus fully on the present moment and find joy in the activity.

- **Positive Distraction**: Hobbies divert your attention away from worries, providing a mental break and reducing rumination.

- **Personal Fulfillment**: Pursuing hobbies can boost your self-esteem and sense of accomplishment as you develop new skills and create something meaningful.

2. Passion:

Passion refers to a deep and intense interest in an activity, subject, or pursuit. When you're passionate about something, you experience a strong emotional connection and intrinsic motivation.

Benefits of Passion:

- **Intrinsic Motivation**: Passion fuels your motivation and drive, making it easier to engage in activities that bring you joy and satisfaction.

- **Stress Resilience**: Pursuing your passions provides a source of resilience that helps you cope with stress and challenges.

- **Positive Emotions**: Engaging in activities you're passionate about can elevate your mood, increase happiness, and reduce negative emotions.

- **Flow State**: Pursuing passions can lead to a state of flow, where you're fully absorbed in the activity, experiencing a sense of timelessness and focus.

3. Play:

Play involves engaging in activities purely for enjoyment, without any specific goal or outcome. Playfulness adds a sense of spontaneity and lightheartedness to your life.

- **Stress Reduction**: Playful activities promote relaxation, laughter, and a sense of fun, all of which contribute to stress reduction.

- **Creativity**: Playfulness fosters creativity and innovative thinking, which can lead to novel solutions for stressors.

- **Social Connection**: Playful interactions with others enhance social bonds, creating a sense of belonging and support.

- **Resilience**: Incorporating play into your routine enhances your ability to bounce back from challenges and setbacks.

Incorporating Hobbies, Passion, and Play:

- **Explore New Interests**: Try out new hobbies or activities to discover what you're passionate about and enjoy.

- **Prioritize Enjoyment**: Engage in activities solely for the joy they bring, rather than focusing on achievement or performance.

- **Make Time For Play**: Integrate playful activities into your routine, whether it's playing games, engaging in creative projects, or enjoying outdoor activities.

- **Set Boundaries**: Dedicate time for your hobbies and passions, creating boundaries to ensure you make time for yourself.

- **Balance and Variety**: Incorporate a mix of hobbies, passions, and play to add variety and flexibility to your stress management routine.

By embracing hobbies, pursuing passions, and incorporating play into your life, you provide yourself with valuable outlets for stress relief, personal fulfillment, and enjoyment. These activities contribute to a more balanced, fulfilling, and resilient approach to stress management and overall well-being.

9.1 The Importance of Leisure and Recreation

Leisure and recreation play a crucial role in stress management, contributing to your overall well-being, relaxation, and quality of life. Engaging in enjoyable and rejuvenating activities during your free time offers numerous physical, mental, and emotional benefits that help counter the negative effects of stress. Here's why leisure and recreation are essential for effective stress management:

1. Stress Reduction:
Leisure activities provide a break from the demands of daily life, allowing you to relax and unwind. Engaging in recreational pursuits helps lower stress hormones and promotes a sense of calm.

2. Mental Refreshment:
Leisure time offers a mental escape from work-related pressures and responsibilities. It allows your mind to rest and rejuvenate, leading to increased focus and mental clarity.

3. Physical Well-Being:
Many recreational activities, such as sports, hiking, and dancing, contribute to physical fitness and health. Regular exercise is a powerful stress reducer that boosts mood and overall vitality.

4. Mood Enhancement:
Engaging in leisure and recreational activities triggers the release of endorphins, neurotransmitters that promote feelings of happiness and well-being.

5. Creativity and Self-Expression:

Pursuing creative hobbies like painting, writing, or playing a musical instrument allows you to express yourself and tap into your creative potential, fostering a sense of accomplishment.

6. Social Interaction:

Participating in recreational activities often involves socializing and connecting with others. Strong social connections are vital for emotional support and stress relief.

7. Mindfulness and Flow:

Engaging in leisure activities promotes mindfulness, where you immerse yourself fully in the present moment. Activities that lead to a state of flow, characterized by intense focus and enjoyment, help alleviate stress.

8. Variety and Novelty:

Trying new leisure activities introduces variety and novelty into your routine, preventing boredom and adding excitement to your life.

9. Work-Life Balance:

Engaging in leisure and recreational activities helps you establish a healthy balance between work and personal life, reducing burnout and promoting well-being.

10. Resilience Building:

Regular leisure and recreation contribute to building resilience, enabling you to better cope with stressors and challenges.

11. Coping Mechanism:
Leisure pursuits provide a healthy outlet for stress, diverting your focus away from worries and allowing you to recharge.

12. Enjoyment and Pleasure:
Engaging in activities you enjoy brings joy and pleasure, promoting a positive mindset and emotional well-being.

13. Improved Sleep Quality:
Engaging in leisure and recreational activities can contribute to better sleep, which is essential for stress recovery.

Incorporating leisure and recreation into your life doesn't have to be complicated or time-consuming. It can involve activities as simple as reading a book, going for a walk, practicing a hobby, or spending quality time with loved ones. By making leisure and recreation a priority, you create opportunities to manage stress, enhance your overall quality of life, and foster a greater sense of balance and well-being.

9.2 Exploring Creative Outlets and Activities

Engaging in creative outlets and activities is a powerful and enjoyable way to manage stress, promote emotional well-being, and enhance your overall quality of life. Creative expression provides a unique channel for processing emotions, reducing tension, and finding joy. Here's how exploring creative outlets can help you manage stress:

1. Self-Expression:
Creative activities allow you to express emotions, thoughts, and ideas that might be difficult to communicate verbally. This can lead to a sense of release and relief.

2. Mindfulness and Flow:
Creative tasks like painting, writing, or crafting can lead to a state of flow, where you're fully absorbed in the activity and experience a sense of timelessness and focus.

3. Stress Reduction:
Engaging in creative activities can lower stress hormones, promote relaxation, and provide a mental break from daily stressors.

4. Emotional Release:
Creative outlets offer a safe space to release pent-up emotions, potentially reducing emotional tension and promoting a sense of catharsis.

5. Problem-Solving and Innovation:

Creativity enhances problem-solving skills by encouraging you to think outside the box and find new perspectives on challenges.

6. Positive Distraction:
Immersing yourself in a creative task redirects your focus away from stressors, reducing rumination and promoting a positive mindset.

7. Sense of Accomplishment:
Completing a creative project can boost self-esteem and a sense of accomplishment, contributing to your overall well-being.

8. Cognitive Engagement:
Engaging in creative activities stimulates cognitive processes, promoting mental agility and keeping your mind sharp.

9. Time For Yourself:
Exploring creative outlets provides dedicated time for self-care and self-expression, which are essential for stress management.

10. Connection With Others:
Participating in creative group activities or sharing your creations with others can foster social connections and a sense of belonging.

Examples of Creative Outlets and Activities:

- **Visual Arts**: Painting, drawing, sketching, coloring, photography, and sculpture.

- **Writing**: Journaling, creative writing, poetry, and storytelling.

- **Crafts**: DIY projects, knitting, crocheting, woodworking, and sewing.

- **Music**: Playing a musical instrument, singing, composing, or listening to music.

- **Performing Arts**: Acting, dancing, theater, and improvisation.

- **Cooking and Baking**: Experimenting with recipes, trying new cooking techniques, and baking.

- **Gardening**: Planting, cultivating, and nurturing plants and flowers.

- **Mindful Coloring**: Engaging in coloring books or mandalas for relaxation.

- **Mindful Crafting**: Creating mindful crafts like origami or mindful coloring.

- **Digital Creations**: Graphic design, digital art, and video editing.

Tips for Exploring Creative Outlets:

- **Start Small**: Begin with a creative activity that interests you and fits your skill level.

- **Make Time**: Dedicate regular time to engaging in creative pursuits, even if it's just a few minutes a day.

- **Be Playful**: Approach your creative activities with a sense of playfulness and curiosity.

- **Embrace Imperfection**: Focus on the process and enjoyment rather than striving for perfection.

- **Experiment**: Try different creative outlets to discover what resonates with you the most.

Exploring creative outlets and activities can be a fulfilling and effective way to manage stress, boost your mood, and foster a deeper connection with yourself. Whether you're creating something visually appealing, expressing your thoughts through writing, or engaging in any other form of creative expression, you're nurturing your well-being and promoting a more balanced and enjoyable life.

9.3 Fostering Personal Growth and Fulfillment

Fostering personal growth is a dynamic and empowering approach to managing stress that involves continuous self-improvement, learning, and development. By focusing on your personal growth journey, you can build resilience, enhance your coping skills, and cultivate a more balanced and fulfilling life. Here's how fostering personal growth contributes to effective stress management:

1. Self-Awareness:
Personal growth begins with self-awareness. Understand your strengths, weaknesses, values, and goals to make informed decisions and respond effectively to stressors.

2. Mindset Shift:

Cultivate a growth mindset, embracing challenges as opportunities for learning and growth rather than as setbacks.

3. Emotional Intelligence:
Enhance your emotional intelligence by developing empathy, managing emotions, and improving your interpersonal skills, which aid in stress management and healthy relationships.

4. Lifelong Learning:
Commit to continuous learning and self-education. Acquiring new knowledge and skills empowers you to face stressors with confidence and adaptability.

5. Resilience Building:
Personal growth strengthens your resilience, enabling you to bounce back from setbacks, adapt to changes, and navigate stressors more effectively.

6. Goal Setting:
Set meaningful and achievable goals that align with your values. Working towards these goals provides a sense of purpose and direction, reducing stress.

7. Positive Habits:
Cultivate positive habits, such as regular exercise, healthy eating, and mindfulness, which contribute to better stress management.

8. Self-Care:

Prioritize self-care practices that nourish your physical, mental, and emotional well-being.

9. Flexibility and Adaptability:
Embrace change and develop the ability to adapt to new circumstances, reducing stress related to unexpected challenges.

10. Mindfulness and Reflection:
Practice mindfulness and regular self-reflection to stay attuned to your thoughts, emotions, and behaviors, fostering self-awareness.

11. Time Management:
Develop effective time management skills to allocate time for work, relaxation, hobbies, and personal growth activities.

12. Communication Skills:
Improve your communication skills to express your needs, set boundaries, and manage conflicts more effectively.

13. Positive Relationships:
Nurture supportive and positive relationships that provide emotional support and contribute to your personal growth.

14. Self-Compassion:
Treat yourself with kindness and understanding, especially during times of stress or challenges.

15. Gratitude and Optimism:
Cultivate gratitude and maintain an optimistic outlook, which enhances your overall well-being and resilience.

Benefits of Fostering Personal Growth:

- **Enhanced Coping**: Personal growth equips you with a diverse range of coping skills, enabling you to handle stressors more effectively.

- **Resilience**: By focusing on personal growth, you become more resilient in the face of challenges and setbacks.

- **Reduced Stress**: Building self-awareness and developing skills contribute to reduced stress and better stress management.

- **Empowerment**: Personal growth empowers you to take charge of your life, make positive changes, and navigate stressors with confidence.

- **Improved Well-Being**: Fostering personal growth leads to an overall improvement in well-being, encompassing physical, mental, and emotional health.

Fostering personal growth is a lifelong journey that involves self-reflection, self-discovery, and continuous effort. By embracing this approach, you create a solid foundation for managing stress, enhancing your resilience, and leading a more meaningful and fulfilling life.

Conclusion: Embracing a Balanced and Stress-Managed Life

On the journey toward a balanced and stress-managed life, you embark on a transformative path of self-discovery, personal growth, and holistic well-being. By integrating a variety of strategies and practices, you empower yourself to navigate the complexities of modern life with resilience, grace, and vitality. Here's a recap of the key elements that contribute to embracing a balanced and stress-managed life:

1. Self-Awareness: Begin by understanding your stress triggers, emotional responses, and personal needs. Self-awareness lays the foundation for effective stress management.

2. Stress Recognition: Develop the ability to recognize the signs of stress in your body, mind, and behavior. This awareness enables timely interventions.

3. Coping Strategies: Cultivate a toolkit of diverse coping strategies, including mindfulness, deep breathing, physical activity, creative expression, and relaxation techniques.

4. Emotional Intelligence: Enhance your emotional intelligence to navigate emotions, build healthy relationships, and respond to stressors with empathy and understanding.

5. Self-Care: Prioritize self-care practices that nourish your physical, mental, and emotional well-being. Make time for activities that bring you joy, relaxation, and fulfillment.

6. Mind-Body Connection: Nurture your well-being by integrating practices that enhance the connection between your mind and body, such as mindfulness, meditation, and exercise.

7. Time Management: Effectively manage your time and set priorities to maintain a balanced schedule that includes work, leisure, personal growth, and relaxation.

8. Communication Skills: Improve your communication skills to express your needs, set boundaries, and foster positive connections with others.

9. Social Support: Build a strong support network of friends, family, and professionals who can provide emotional guidance and encouragement.

10. Resilience: Develop resilience through personal growth, adaptive coping strategies, and a positive mindset that enables you to bounce back from challenges.

11. Play and Creativity: Engage in hobbies, creative outlets, and play to infuse your life with joy, spontaneity, and a sense of wonder.

12. Work-Life Balance: Strive for a healthy balance between work, personal time, and relaxation to prevent burnout and maintain a fulfilling lifestyle.
13. Growth Mindset: Embrace a growth mindset that views challenges as opportunities for learning, growth, and self-improvement.

14. Gratitude and Optimism: Cultivate gratitude and maintain an optimistic outlook to foster a positive mindset and enhance overall well-being.

15. Mindfulness: Practice mindfulness to stay present, manage stress, and develop a deeper connection with yourself and the world around you.

16. Continuous Learning: Commit to ongoing learning and personal development, expanding your knowledge, skills, and perspectives.

As you weave these elements into the fabric of your daily life, you create a harmonious tapestry of well-being, resilience, and fulfillment. Embracing a balanced and stress-managed life isn't about eliminating stress entirely; it's about equipping yourself with the tools and mindset to navigate it with grace and confidence. Through this journey, you'll find yourself better equipped to savor life's joys, overcome challenges, and embrace each moment with a sense of purpose and tranquility.

Appendix: Resources and Tools for Continued Stress Management

Managing stress is an ongoing journey that requires continuous effort and exploration. Here are some valuable resources and tools to support your continued stress management efforts:

1. Recommended Books:

- "The Relaxation and Stress Reduction Workbook" by Martha Davis, Elizabeth Robbins Eshelman, and Matthew McKay

- "The Mindful Path to Self-Compassion" by Christopher Germer

- "Emotional Intelligence" by Daniel Goleman

- "Atomic Habits" by James Clear"

- "The Upside of Stress: Why Stress Is Good for You and How to Get Good at It" by Kelly McGonigal

- "Daring Greatly: How the Courage to Be Vulnerable Transforms the Way We Live, Love, Parent, and Lead" by Brené Brown

- "The Power of Now: A Guide to Spiritual Enlightenment" by Eckhart Tolle

- "Radical Acceptance: Embracing Your Life with the Heart of a Buddha" by Tara Brach

2. Recommended Apps:

- Headspace: Offers guided meditation and mindfulness exercises.

- Calm: Provides meditation, relaxation techniques, and sleep stories.

- Insight Timer: Offers a wide range of meditation practices and mindfulness resources.

- Moodfit: Helps track and manage moods, stress, and emotional well-being.

- MyLife Meditation (formerly Stop, Breathe, and Think): Provides meditation and mindfulness activities tailored to your emotional state.

- Happify: Offers activities and games designed to boost happiness and resilience.

- SuperBetter: Helps you build resilience and achieve personal goals through gamified challenges.

3. Online Courses:

- Coursera and Udemy offer courses on stress management, mindfulness, emotional intelligence, and personal growth.

4. Recommended Websites:

- Mindful (www.mindful.org): Offers articles, guided meditations, and resources for mindfulness and stress reduction.

- HelpGuide (www.helpguide.org): Provides information and practical advice on managing stress, anxiety, and other mental health topics.

- TED Talks (www.ted.com): Explore talks on stress, resilience, happiness, and personal growth.

- PsychCentral: (www.psychcentral.com)

- Provides a range of articles and resources related to mental health, stress management, and personal growth.

- Greater Good Magazine: (greatergood.berkeley.edu)

- Offers science-based articles and tools for well-being, happiness, and stress reduction.

- Tiny Buddha: (tinybuddha.com): Features articles, quotes, and stories on mindfulness, personal growth, and well-being.

- Positive Psychology (positivepsychology.com): Provides research-based articles and resources on positive psychology, happiness, and resilience.

5. Professional Support:

- Consider seeking guidance from a licensed therapist, counselor, or psychologist for personalized stress management strategies.

6. Meditation and Relaxation Resources:

- Guided meditation videos on YouTube and meditation apps.

- Relaxation exercises, deep breathing techniques, and progressive muscle relaxation.

7. Physical Activity Resources:

- Online workout videos, fitness apps, or joining local fitness classes

- Nature walks, hiking, jogging, and other outdoor activities

8. Create Outlets and Hobbies:

- Art supply stores, craft workshops, and local community centers.

- Online tutorials for painting, drawing, crafting, or playing a musical instrument

9. Time Management Tools:

- Productivity apps like Todoist, Trello, or Google Calendar.

- Time management techniques like the Pomodoro Technique

10. Social Support and Connection:

- Join social groups, clubs, or community events to connect with like-minded individuals.

- Reach out to friends, family, or support groups for emotional support.

11. Work-Life Balance Resources:

- Online articles, podcasts, and workshops on work-life balance strategies

12. Mindfulness and Mind-Body Practices:

- Yoga classes, tai chi, and mindfulness retreats

- Mindfulness-based stress reduction (MBSR) programs

Remember, each person's journey to managing stress is unique. Explore different resources, tools, and techniques to discover what resonates with you and supports your well-being. Regularly revisit and update your stress management strategies as you continue to learn and grow.

Please note that the availability and effectiveness of these resources may vary. Always prioritize your safety and consult with a healthcare professional if you have any concerns about your mental or physical health.

Worksheets and Exercises for Practicing Stress Management Techniques

Here are some worksheets and exercises that can help you practice various stress management techniques:

1. Deep Breathing Exercise:

- Worksheet: Deep Breathing Worksheet

- Exercise:

    - Find a quiet and comfortable place to sit or lie down.

    - Close your eyes and take a deep breath in through your nose, filling your lungs completely.

    - Hold your breath for a few seconds.

    - Slowly exhale through your mouth, releasing all the air from your lungs.

    - Repeat this deep breathing pattern for several minutes, focusing on your breath and letting go of tension.

2. Mindfulness Meditation:

- Worksheet: Mindfulness Meditation Journal

- Exercise:

  - Sit or lie down in a comfortable position.

  - Focus your attention on your breath or a specific sensation in your body.

  - Notice any thoughts, feelings, or sensations that arise without judgment.

  - Gently redirect your focus back to your breath or sensation whenever your mind starts to wander.

  - Practice this mindfulness meditation for a few minutes each day, gradually increasing the duration.

3. Progressive Muscle Relaxation:

- Worksheet: Progressive Muscle Relaxation Guide

- Exercise:

  - Sit or lie down in a comfortable position.

  - Start with your toes and tense the muscles in that area for a few seconds.

  - Release the tension and focus on the sensation of relaxation.

  - Gradually work your way up through different muscle groups, tensing and relaxing each one.

  - Pay attention to the contrast between tension and relaxation as you move through your body.

4. Gratitude Journaling:

- Worksheet: Gratitude Journal

- Exercise:

- Set aside a few minutes each day to write down three things you're grateful for.

- Reflect on both big and small moments of gratitude.

- Describe why each thing you're grateful for is important to you.

- Over time, this practice can help shift your focus towards positive aspects of your life and reduce stress.

5. Time Management and Prioritization:

- Worksheet: Time Management Planner

- Exercise:

  - List your daily tasks and responsibilities.

  - Prioritize tasks based on their importance and deadlines.

- Allocate time blocks for each task in your schedule.

- Stick to your planned schedule and adjust as needed.

- Reflect on how effective your time management was at the end of the day.

6. Relaxation Techniques:

- Worksheet: Relaxation Techniques Practice Log

- Exercise:

  - Choose a relaxation technique such as visualization, guided imagery, or nature walks.

  - Practice the chosen technique for a set amount of time each day.

- Use the log to track your practice and note any changes in your stress levels.

Remember, consistent practice is key to experiencing the full benefits of these techniques. Customize the worksheets and exercises to suit your preferences and needs. If you find it challenging to practice on your own, consider seeking guidance from a therapist or counselor who can provide personalized support and guidance.